LEADING WITH
GRATITUDE !

Seth Breckley

Gaz 2:20

ENDORSEMENTS

"Seth Buechley challenges us to imagine a world where we go to work thinking about how grateful we are for our jobs, how grateful we are for the opportunity to lead, and how grateful we are for the fruits of our labor. Gratefulness leads us to think of others more often than ourselves—and the rewards fill up our souls in a powerful way. Don't miss this life-changing insight."

Cheryl A. Bachelder
CEO, Popeyes Louisiana Kitchen, Inc.,
and Author, *Dare to Serve*

"With his wonderfully written book, *Ambition*, Seth provides an insightful understanding of the forces that drive and, all too often, destroy entrepreneurs. His careful blending of applied business, psychology, and philosophy is unique and missing in our education. Seth's book should become required annual reading for entrepreneurs and those living with them!"

Harry Clark
CEO, Pathway Partners, and Author,
Mistakes Millionaires Make

"Ambition is like having a brick in your hand. It can be used to smash windows or to build cathedrals. Unbridled ambition can destroy dreams and lives. This book will show you how to harness your ambition through experience, integrity, and hard work in a way that will leave a positive legacy and improve the world."

Dan Miller
New York Times bestselling author,
48 Days to the Work You Love

"*Ambition* is a powerful book on understanding how a focus on gratitude can boost leadership impact and overall satisfaction in your life. Required reading for high achievers who want to fuel their professional and personal successes while fully enjoying the journey at the same time. I highly recommend this book for anyone who would self-identify as an ambitious leader."

Don Antonucci
President, Regence BlueShield

"Seth Buechley, via a series of his own successes and failures, helps ambitious leaders hit the reset button to avoid the crash that so frequently follows success. He shifts our focus from temporal goal achievement to development of eternal values and relationships and moves our expectations from seeking success to leaving a legacy of thankfulness. *Ambition* is a must read for leaders, especially those who have reached the top and are thinking, 'Is this all there is?'"

Merrill Oster
Entrepreneur and Founder, Pinnacle Forum

"While examining many (often self-created) problems for people with ambition, Seth Buechley offers solutions with humility, humor, and insight. *Ambition* serves not only as a window into the life of a self-made multi-millionaire who was raised in a commune, it also provides thoughtful reflection and insight on how to productively channel the drive of go-getters. I was compelled to look into my own drive, ambitions, and life."

Toby Luther
President and CEO, Lone Rock Resources

"As an executive speaker coach, I get an opportunity to come alongside executives in some of the largest and most successful companies in America. For some of those leaders, however, success has been unkind. Seth Buechley gives us a unique look into the trait of ambition and offers every hard-charging leader a simple remedy for the burnout they sooner or later experience."

Jim Endicott
President, Distinction Communications

"A captivating and inspiring book that reads like an entrepreneur's devotional. *Ambition* is the antidote to the overwhelming pressure leaders face."

Evan Loomis
Author, *Get Backed*

"Speaking for most seasoned entrepreneurs, I am sure we all would have liked to have read *Ambition* before having to learn these similar lessons on our own journeys. If you experience early success, don't let your ego and pride blind you to believing you will have equal success in different types of ventures. As Seth Buechley shares, the sooner you find gratitude in all you do, the sooner you will find true purpose and meaningful success. This book will save ambitious entrepreneurs much pain by following these practical steps of experiencing gratitude, finding true purpose, and creating impact for others. The results will be a legacy your family will be proud of."

John Hall
CEO, 16 Degree Advisory and Innate Guidance Systems

"*Ambition* drives people in business, but also in non-profits, government, and even family life. But driven where? Buechley points toward a kind of modern nirvana—not the false kind he saw growing up in a commune, but the real satisfaction that comes from gratitude for what we have. He warns against the eternal longing the ambitious endure for what we want—which is never satisfied, no matter how much we achieve. There is no greater gift than what his book offers: peace of mind for those among us who suffer from the ambition gene, while increasing—not diminishing—our effectiveness at changing our world for the better."

Jonathan Adelstein
President and CEO, Wireless Infrastructure Association

"Having just sold a business and moving toward the next chapter in my life, I found the pages of *Ambition: Leading with Gratitude* to be speaking directly to me. I think you will find this book a challenge to motivate you to do more than simply succeed in whatever you pursue, but to influence others and create a legacy along the way. I highly recommend this book!"

James W. Kramer
President, Legacy Wireless Services, Inc., and Founder, FASTER Cycling Performance Center

"I had concluded long ago that ambitious people like me are often unhappy people, never satisfied with the way things are. We always think we can improve the situation, and as soon as we do, we forget that improvement and move on to the next challenge. This book teaches us the first step to quiet that endless inner angst, while still recognizing the important and proper place of ambition in our lives."

Alan Gates
Co-Founder, Hortonworks

"Thank you Seth Buechley for *Ambition*. It not only felt as if this book was written for me, but it was also delivered at the perfect time in my life. Whether you are igniting your first start-up, in the midst of building a large company, or wondering what to do next…this book is an absolute must-read."

J. T. Service
Founder and CEO, Soul Focus Sports

"This is a valuable read if you are a person who wants to be a great business leader and develop positive and lasting relationships with the most important people in your life. *Ambition* is full of many easy-to-execute insights such as creating your own process for a 'gratitude adjustment' or intentionally thinking about ways to leave a positive legacy before it is too late. As a husband, father, and CEO of a sports and entertainment organization, I found the book to be applicable to all aspects of my daily life."

Chris McGowan
President and CEO, Portland Trail Blazers

"*Ambition* reads like you're talking over coffee with Seth Buechley. Humble, soulful, insightful, and full of gems, the wisdom comes alongside you through the pages. I highly recommend this book to the first-time entrepreneur, the mid-career professional considering making a move, or the seasoned leader who is thinking about mentoring."

Jason A. Atkinson
Former Oregon State Senator, Candidate for Governor,
Filmmaker, Writer, Entrepreneur

"Seth Buechley artfully shares his journey of personal resilience. In *Ambition*, he shows us how we can not only become a successful businessperson, but a successful human."

Tracy Maddux
CEO, CD Baby

"I'd like to go back and give my '23-year-old-self' the book *Ambition*! Seth Buechley strikes the right balance between storytelling and hard-learned wisdom. The book is sure to help would-be leaders blend the desire to 'be and do something important' with the values and guardrails that ensure the journey is guided by integrity and framed with humility and honesty. *Ambition* is a must-read for anyone who wants to do something big but wants to cut 10 years off learning how to do it right."

Keith Thomajan
President and CEO, United Way of the Columbia-Willamette

"I met Seth Buechley 15 years ago, but I now realize I didn't really know him until I read *Ambition* on a recent flight. The story of his unusual upbringing is, alone, worth the read! Ambition is not an easy topic to handle; a lesser author could have offended his readers with arrogance, or worse, wasted their time with platitudes. Buechley, writing with grace and humor, caused this skeptic to stop repeatedly to ponder his insights on gratitude. I dare you to read *Ambition* and not make a gift list of certain friends and colleagues who would benefit from its pages."

F. Howard Mandel
President, Peppertree Capital Management, Inc.

"Seth Buechley takes us on a fascinating journey of life through his book, *Ambition*. A journey of ambition and how ambition can magnify someone's career, professional, and even their personal life. The magnification of the virtue of ambition he points out can be rewarding and fulfilling, but there are times that ambition can result in destruction. He shares with us the key to successfully harnessing one's ambition, determination, and achieving the goals in front of us is to embrace the values of contentment, peace, gratitude, and patience. These oftentimes are difficult traits to learn and even harder to practice. Buechley may have handed us the very simple keys to happiness. This book is for everyone, especially for young adults entering into their professional careers."

Christine M. Stoffel

CEO and Founder, SEAT LLC, SEAT Europe LLC, Silicon Sports Accelerator LLC, iLead-SE LLC, and CBR Sports Group LLC

"In an industry replete with leaders who are put to the ultimate test daily, we know which ones are good when we see them. With his book, *Ambition*, Seth Buechley has distinguished himself as one such leader. This book strikes at the core of effective leadership. Truly a rare glimpse into self-reflection and personal growth."

Jeffrey D. Johnson

Fire Chief (Ret.), CEO, Western Fire Chiefs Association, and Past President, International Association of Fire Chiefs

"*Ambition: Leading with Gratitude* is one of the best leadership books I've read in years. In pointing out a very simple truth, the importance of gratitude to our personal happiness and to our ability to lead others effectively, Seth Buechley contributes greatly to our understanding of true leadership and its relevance in our work and lives."

Rob Miller
President, Trailblazer Foods and President,
Miller Family Foundation

"Stephen Covey's Habit 5 'Seek first to understand, then to be understood' comes to life in Seth Buechley's *Ambition: Leading with Gratitude*. As a public safety professional for more than 36 years, I have had the opportunity to interact with many types of personalities in some very trying circumstances. I often wondered why what I'll term 'really ambitious people' were not more grateful in some of those situations. Now I know. Buechley not only brings a deep understanding of the ambitious mindset that will help every reader understand where they are coming from, but also where they will want to go. The insights within this book provide some exceptional direction that you can put to work to improve your family life and career."

Chief Alan Perdue (Ret.)
Director, Guilford County Emergency Services

"Too many times, I caught myself smiling and nodding my head in agreement to the 'almost always anxious' trait that plagues me and many other leaders. Seth Buechley has captured, near perfectly, the state of those of us whom identify as 'ambitious' and has given all of us a road map to contentment. *Ambition* is a playbook for learning how to embrace our inner drive, in a healthy way, to find greater fulfillment in life."

Robb Crocker
CEO, Funnelbox Inc., and
Author, *Stock Footage Millionaire*

"Seth Buechley has taken a unique and circuitous route to such an intuitive place as a business man and entrepreneur. He details with adroitness his early life on a commune, working with his father to become very successful and rather wealthy at a young age. His book is festooned with memorable quotes, such as, 'Comparison is the thief of joy'—Teddy Roosevelt. I believe anyone who fancies themselves as an entrepreneur, or who would like to become one, would find this book to be a treasure trove of insight and real-life observations. There are nuggets here for everyone."

Peb Jackson
Principal, Jackson Consulting Group LLC

"Why is it so hard to connect the good stuff like ambition, smarts, connections, spirit, education, etc. and parlay into lasting gold? This universal quandary is thoroughly addressed in thousands of business, psychology, and self-help books. Some are great, some are fire starters. I'll be darned if that kid Seth Buechley didn't write one of the best wisdom texts I've ever read. With characteristic confidence, a measure of humility, intelligence, and woodsy candor, *Ambition: Leading with Gratitude* explores who we are (your name here), peers gently into ambitious faults, illuminates escape routes to fulfillment, and most importantly, promotes personal/communal growth through the inherent power of gratitude. I wish I'd written it."

Mike McWhirter
President and CEO, CBA Site Services, Inc.

"There are many books on business recipe, but very few are talking about the art of appreciation. *Ambition* is putting the real values of successful businesses in the right order while sharing good and bad experiences where most entrepreneurs will recognize themselves. Easy and fun to read, *Ambition* was like a new high-tech startup… innovative and different."

Mario Bouchard
Co-Founder, iBwave, Ernst & Young Entrepreneur of the Year, Quebec IT October 2011

"Life is the ultimate team game, and the lessons I found in *Ambition* will go a long way to making one's chosen endeavors or life pursuits a more rewarding and meaningful experience."

Ross Manire
Chairman and CEO, ExteNet Systems, Inc.

"*Ambition* perfectly breaks down why we high-achieving entrepreneurs and leaders struggle with the "pursuit of achievement" vs. the "pursuit of happiness"...and how to finally find lasting satisfaction, happiness, impact, and legacy while we're making big things happen. Seth absolutely nails it on why we tend to struggle with satisfaction when we're achieving at our highest levels... and lays out a clear framework for dealing with our ambition that is simple, powerful, and crazy effective. Read the book, it's a simple concept that could change your outlook on life and business."

Trevor Mauch
CEO, Carrot, and Top 100 Young Entrepreneurs
Under 35 in America (Empact100)

"I am the lawyer that Seth mentions in the book that he sometimes listens to and sometimes doesn't. I just completed *Ambition*; I loved and hated it. When I hated it was when Seth held up the mirror to shine a light on my own drive for success. I was most impacted by the sections on ambition vs. satisfaction. What is enough? How do we channel the drive we have for success into something good instead of something that separates us from our family or other human interaction? *Ambition* will serve to help me implement gratitude into the way I lead."

Coni Rathbone
Co-Founder and Shareholder,
Zupancic Rathbone Law Group, PC

"Seth has captured the essence of ambitious people/entrepreneurs in this book, calling them addictive, ambitious, bold, creative, curious, determined, driven, full of personal flaws, having a high-rejection tolerance, independent, impatient, intolerant, insatiable, lacking empathy, lacking self-awareness, laser focused, rules averse, and visionary, but seldom happy. He then provides a road map to how such people can achieve greater happiness and satisfaction if they are willing to change and become grateful, focusing on others and not just on themselves."

John Castles
Trustee, MJ Murdock Charitable Trust

AMBITION

Leading with Gratitude

SETH BUECHLEY

elevate

Editorial Work: AnnaMarie McHargue
Cover Design: Aaron Snethen
Layout Design: Aaron Snethen
Cover Photography:
   www.unsplash.com:
   Anthony.Delanoix- New York City Skyscrapers

   www.pexels.com:
   Annie Spratt- Back of Kid

Published in Boise, Idaho by Elevate. An imprint of Elevate
Publishing.

This book may be purchased in bulk for educational,
business, organizational, or promotional use.

For information, please email info@elevatepub.com

Hardback ISBN-13: 9781943425839

eBook ISBN-13: 9781943425846

Library of Congress Control Number: 2016942587

Printed in the United States of America

DEDICATION

To Sally Leahy, my high school English teacher, who encouraged me to keep writing. To Phil Clements, who chose investment in others over the comfortable life. And, finally, to my dad, Mark Buechley, an intentional mentor and loving father who passed during the writing of this book. He was my best friend.

CONTENTS

INTRODUCTION

Sure, I hope this book sells a million copies. But, *more importantly*, I hope this book prevents a million tears in the lives of the ambitious people who read it and share it with others.

To be clear upfront, I don't view ambition as a negative trait. In fact, I don't think anything important gets done without somebody, usually an ambitious person, getting agitated enough to take action. But we must not overlook the downside of risks high achievers face as they take on the world. In 25 years of business ventures, I've seen a lot of talented leaders completely self-destruct because they didn't get their ambition under control. Unfortunately, when a leader crashes and burns, it doesn't happen in a vacuum. The collateral damage to their family and the companies they lead is tremendous. As an entrepreneur wired to challenge and build, I've experienced wonderful opportunities and accomplishments. I've also experienced serious anxiety, crushing disappointments, and a variety of self-inflicted wounds that could have been avoided.

The central idea we'll explore in this book is the powerful effect gratitude can have in the lives of ambitious people. Experts contend that practicing gratitude has the greatest impact on those who previously had been the least grateful. In my experience, however, ambitious people are often those who are *least grateful*. The good news is this can be remedied! The earlier, the better.

This book is written to help ambitious people discover more satisfaction and purpose in the midst of their pursuits. Chapters 1-5 provide an **Understanding** of what fuels our ambition and the many pitfalls we face. In Chapter 6, we focus on the single biggest **Change** ambitious people need to make in order to live a life with greater contentment and satisfaction. Chapter 7 challenges us to dig deeper to get clear on our motivations and **Purpose**. And, finally, Chapters 8-10 suggest three areas of **Focus** for achieving lasting leadership impact.

Writing a book had been a vision of mine since high school. It took me a few decades to figure out exactly what I wanted to say. Of course, the pace of life as a family man and entrepreneur provided many reasons why it just "wasn't the right time." As speaking and coaching opportunities increased, the message I have for ambitious high achievers crystalized to the point I knew it was finally time to share the message through a book. As the title implies, the book targets people who consider themselves ambitious. Our media-rich culture bombards us with messages about success, achievement, and wealth. Ambition, determination, accomplishments, goals…these are well-worn stones we carry in our pocket as we journey to make our mark in the world. But what about contentment, peace, gratitude, and patience? Are these softer virtues? Whether softer or not, we can likely agree that they aren't natural virtues for many driven personality types. They have to be intentionally cultivated and developed.

I meet a lot of up-and-coming entrepreneurs and business leaders. I'm often impressed with their innovation in

creating intentional organizations and dynamic businesses that ride current trends and waves of technology. But
I've paid attention and observed a darker side of ambition
that can slowly cloud any leader's vision and drive their
train off the rails, no matter how noble or well-intended
their cause. I hope to provide ambitious people with some
practical tools to help prevent their ambition from turning destructive.

I also wrote *Ambition* to leave my children and grand-
children with a clearer understanding of my worldview,
and to challenge them to harness their ambition for the
benefit of others. What they may not recall from our conversations, they will be able to reference from a book-
shelf. It's been lamented that the first generation builds
something valuable, the second generation gets spoiled to
the point they have soft *hands*, and the third generation is
spoiled to the point they have soft *heads*. It doesn't have to
be like that! I am determined that it won't be, and I know
it starts with me.

Trends and the cultural definitions of success may
change, but human nature and the transformative power
of gratitude are unchanging. I hope this book will cause
you to stop and think; to ask yourself hard questions
about what drives you, and to develop your own relationship with gratitude.

Seth Buechley
Roseburg, OR

CHAPTER 1
Roots of Ambition

I knew the *meeting* would eventually turn to me. While the other kids from the commune were distracted with television or games, I quietly made my way to the office located above the great dining room where meetings were always held. A dusty air vent at the base of the wall would allow me to hear most of the proceedings and provide a partial view of the adults sitting around the massive wood table that accommodated several dozen people comfortably. The commune leaders at *Living Springs* called meetings to discuss important issues. Members of the commune, or at least those at my family's level, were required to be there, all gathered around the grand table that had a hand-painted scene of Christ's Last Supper spread across its width. Earlier that day, I was involved in a heated argument with a friend that ended with some serious mocking—and his tears. He was in junior high, a few years older than I was and, evidently, I expected him to be able to hold his own. I failed to anticipate what would happen if he went home crying to his mom. That's how I became a key talking point in that meeting's agenda.

In a traditional court of law, each party has representation and gets to tell his side of the story. In the commune, justice was administered differently. From my perch above the gathering of adults, I heard my name and the overview of the conflict from earlier in the day. Judgments about my character were pronounced. I was described as a "trouble-maker," a "button-pusher" with a long history of being a bad kid. I was crushed. The judgment was more than I was willing to bear. How could I face these adults the next day, knowing what they really thought of me?

DRIVEN BY OUR DYSFUNCTION

We are all driven by our dysfunction to some degree. Whether trauma, drama, or the struggles of this life, no one gets through unscathed. Eventually, though, most of us begin to question what makes us tick. Looking back, I know many of the key drivers that shape my personality were formed in the 17 years I spent in the commune in Southern Oregon. I recall my burning tears and anger following the meeting described above. My internal sense of justice had been violated, and I refused to accept the judgment of these adults based on one-sided testimony. I didn't claim complete innocence regarding the argument I'd had, but I knew that this system was rigged and that I was no longer willing to be part of it. Give me some time and a fair shot, and I'd achieve something great. Just watch.

The experiences of these formative years certainly played out later in my life, but this book is not intended as a biography. It's more of a "why-ography," an exploration of what motivates highly ambitious people and the pitfalls and opportunities you'll likely encounter on your journey.

To be clear, life in the commune wasn't all bad. (Actually, I had to write that so my mom will keep reading.)

"We are all **driven by** our **dysfunction** to some degree."

When the founder of the commune left Los Angeles, he couldn't have picked a more idyllic piece of property than our 80 acres of beautiful valley land surrounded by the fir-laden mountains for which Southern Oregon is famous. A small creek running through the middle of the property provided necessary irrigation and all the crawfish hunting young boys could ask for. In the late 60s and early 70s, up to 1,000 communes (hippie and otherwise) cropped up all over the U.S. And, in fact, there were still about 100 known communes across America still in existence by the 90s.[i] In the case of *Living Springs*, the founder was a former professional wrestler who claimed a call from God to start a children's home for those who needed help getting on the right track. That vision morphed into a commune over a few years, and the population of *Living Springs*, most commonly called the *Valley*, fluctuated between 40 and 80 people with a steady flow of visitors and guests joining and leaving the half dozen families, like mine, who lived on site permanently. Those who came to the commune, including my parents, generally had difficult family backgrounds and were seeking the fatherly oversight of the commune leader and the strong sense of community fostered by living with "all things in common." Many had life-changing positive experiences that formed their identity and worldview, particularly in the early years before the predicable drift away from equality toward authoritarianism.

Family life was a hybrid of normal parental authority with an overlay of authority held by the commune leader. Kids were required to listen to our parents, and our parents were required to live within the will and guidance of the commune—and especially its leader. Dinner was served nightly in the *Big House,* a massive barn-like structure positioned prominently at the end of the long dirt road that meandered alongside the creek, guiding visitors from the interstate up into the valley with mile-high King Mountain looming in the distance. The *ladies,* as they were called, took turns preparing and serving dinner cafeteria-style. Breakfast and lunch were served in our family homes, which were scattered randomly across the *Valley.* With a dozen or more kids living on the property, there was always a long list of chores to be done, ranging from weeding the garden, to cleaning the shops, to milking the cows. Truth be told, there was also a lot of normal kid fun and fond memories.

While we didn't have a lot of focused family time around the dinner table or normal family vacations, we had plenty of stuff to make us feel Southern Oregon middle-class. Most of us boys had motorcycles and thousands of nearby acres of forest to explore. A skateboard park, rope swing, full exercise gym, and an indoor swimming pool made it hard to feel like we were suffering for material stuff. We attended the public schools of the nearby town that was anchored by two small lumber mills providing the scarce jobs that kept some sort of economic activity in an area that otherwise might have been unnoticed by drivers making the trek between San Francisco and Portland.

One of the unwritten values of our commune leader, and therefore, the commune, was workaholism. The men worked nearly nonstop as builders, sometimes on the road for weeks on end, at job sites throughout the west.

All wages and project profits were pooled together and used to fund the operations of the commune. That's not to say that funds were shared equally. In the *Valley*, the caste-system was very much at work, and power over financial decisions was retained by the commune leader and his blood relatives. Other members of the commune had to negotiate permission to go visit their own relatives and even to receive them as guests.

Looking back, I know now the commune, regardless of how it was intended or how it may have functioned in the early years, became a cult. Not primarily a religious cult, but mostly a personality cult orbiting the ego of a shorter-than-average leader with an insatiable appetite to control and dominate others. There was no room for the success of others, no ideas better than his own, and no freedom to debate and decide one's own future. People who study cult behavior universally observe a practice called *jangling*—the random promotion and demotion of individuals for the purpose of creating instability. I witnessed years of jangling as commune members were recognized and promoted by the leader for their 60 seconds in the sun, only to be attacked and brought low or pitted against others in the coming days. Even husbands and wives were wedged apart, creating a small group of divorced women dependent upon the commune for their very survival. Only the leader and his immediate family could stay on top for any sustained period of time. That's just the way it was.

Fortunately, in my case, my parents were very loving and committed to their family. My father, within the structure of the commune, built a successful business special-

izing in removing trees from around power lines. A ridic-
ulously hard worker, he was also an intentional mentor
and entrepreneur, challenging me to resist the standard
institutional storyline and pursue whatever alternate path
I chose. After all, he left home at 17 to participate in the
cultural upheaval of the 60s. His stories included resisting the Vietnam draft, living in the San Francisco Bay
Area, the hippie epicenter, and even a brief stint in a cor-
rectional institution as a result of trying his hand at international smuggling! I have great memories of riding in
the pickup truck going to and from work with my father
as he shared stories of his anti-establishment youth.

In the commune, lack of education was worn as a macho
badge of honor. The anti-education bias fed into the myth
fostered by the commune leader that he was a "self-made"
success. Being self-made is, of course, made easier when
one has a cadre of unpaid workers helping the cause. My
dad simply didn't believe formal education provided the
primary keys to a successful life. In his mind, formal education was a place where people often hid from reality.
His perspective, no doubt, was colored heavily by the
fact that his distant, disengaged father, whom he fled as
a teenager, was an academic who served as a professor of
epidemiology at the University of California in Berkeley.

UNCHARTED WATERS

We all get launched into life from somewhere. I was
launched from a commune. At 17, my parents finally
decided enough was enough and decided to leave *Living
Springs* and the idea of communal living. At 40 years old,

after working for over a decade to build the tree-trimming business that brought millions of dollars of revenue into the commune, my father agreed to buy the business from the commune for $40,000. The problem was that our family was leaving the commune with *nothing* but a van. He lacked the personal assets to collateralize a meaningful loan.

This proved to be one of those moments that validated one of my father's basic premises on life—you can't figure everything out before you start. You start, then you uncover and solve the problems as you go. The key is in the starting. You can't *know* until you *go*. We went.

This lesson reinforces one of my guiding philosophies as an entrepreneur. The first person to the uncharted waters gets to make the charts.

After being turned down by a local bank because he had no real assets, he reached out to a customer several hours away who had become a good friend. This friend managed a power company in another county and was willing to introduce his local banking contacts and personally vouch for my dad. The loan came through. We were finally free to chart our own course.

A NEW BEGINNING

Initially, our family chose to remain in the same town after leaving the commune. With one elementary school, one junior high, and one high school, we'd been with our classmates since we had baby teeth. We enjoyed some successful sports campaigns, and our wrestling team, which I was involved with, was a perennial top-tier

"The first person to the **uncharted waters** gets to **make the charts.**"

competitor for our school size. I was elected incoming student body president my junior year, but, before my senior year began, the school canceled nearly all sports and extracurricular activities due to a budget shortfall. This was our chance to break ties with the community once and for all. Sports were a big part of what kept our heads in the game with regard to schooling, so, in a matter of months, we made the decision to relocate to scenic Glide, Oregon, a small town resting at the base of the pristine Umpqua National Forest. Glide is known as the home of Colliding Rivers Park, where a little river named... wait for it...Little River collides head-on with the larger North Umpqua River, famous for its world-class fly fishing.

The students in Glide also had one elementary, one junior high, and one high school. They'd been together since kindergarten, and I was the new guy showing up for senior year. I pledged to lay low while I figured out the new landscape, but then jumped right into "daily-double" football practices and made the varsity football team, weighing in at a whopping 135 lbs.

Somewhere within those first few weeks floating around the campus of Glide High School, I spotted *her*. Helen, with the namesake of her grandmother Helene, had spent her entire life in the small town. The youngest of three sisters, Helen was raised up at Cavitt Creek (or "crick" in some places) on a country farm under the afternoon shadows of the kind of mountain scenes giving rise to the Hundred Valleys of the Umpqua moniker. Despite the rural farm upbringing, and a father with a John Wayne persona, she was the baby of the family who could never suppress her inner princess. She was beautiful and a *good girl*. I was smitten.

A few weeks into the school year, I pronounced to a friend that I would be dating Helen within six months. He couldn't help observing that I was "very cocky," especially for being the new guy. She did have the small matter of an older boyfriend...but *I would not be deterred*. In a matter of weeks, we were dating. Seventeen months after graduating high school, we were married in a country church surrounded by a small gathering of friends and family. This year, we celebrated 25 years of marriage.

After high school, my father presented me with an interesting challenge as I tried to decide between college and working in a new business he had started. "Do you want to go to school or be a millionaire by the time you're 25?" he asked. He was challenging me to join with him in building a business. Starting at the bottom, of course.

The question for me wasn't all that difficult: I had resented the institutional structure of my early school years. It seemed to me that the information we were learning could be exchanged in about a third of the time. I truly felt public education was a social experiment gone bad. I enjoyed learning and could compete academically when I felt like it, but, for the most part, I disliked school. I used to skip class with a nine iron and hit balls from goalpost to goalpost, scheming how to exit school early. In junior high, I even met with a guidance counselor to see what I could do in order to graduate early. His answer was, "Nothing." I was trapped, so I made the best of it by focusing on sports and friends. I only debated about attending college because so many people had suggested to me that I had to go in order to be successful. But, in my core, I believed that while that may apply to others, it didn't apply to me. Of course, as an entrepreneur-type with a contrarian bias, I felt that way about most things. If they had taken any time at all to understand how I was wired or recognize my entrepreneurial tendencies, they might have pitched college as a place to obtain skills, resources, and connections that would help me serve and solve problems down the road. Instead, today, many school leaders sell college as the primary path to "success." In reality, I've discovered there are many disillusioned folks with expensive degrees struggling to make student loan payments from low-wage jobs.

FINDING OUR WAY

Within a year of graduating high school, and before Helen and I were married, I also discovered where I stood in the "faith department." That personal experience reshaped my view of the world and challenged my own motivation for attending college, which, at the time, had more to do with playing than it did with learning. So, instead of college at the University of Oregon, I threw myself into two main areas of activity: serving a small church as a youth leader and working with my dad in a new business focused on building infrastructure for cellular networks.

Stated simply, we built cellular towers. My dad, perceiving a lack of interest from his sons in cutting trees for a living, started a construction company and named the new business CORD Communications using an acronym of the names of the sons who might be involved. I began working for CORD right out of high school as a laborer, literally digging ditches, pouring concrete, and erecting towers up and down the West Coast. It was an exciting time, and I was pushed into greater areas of responsibility every day as we grew our business. The projects involved short, intense timelines and a lot of moving components. Eventually, I became a 33 percent stakeholder in the business when another shareholder decided he'd had enough of the cowboy-entrepreneur life and decided to leave the business and sell his ownership to my father and me. The price was $1, which says something about his confidence in where we were headed.

I spent that time learning how to understand and work with my dad. He was a visionary—the big picture guy. I would tell people that he was the grand marshal at the front of the parade and I was the "pooper-scooper" following the horses with a shovel. He drove progress, and I focused on business development and business processes. Many times, I would meet people for the first time, and they would tell me how highly my dad had spoken of me. Even though there were some heated moments in the grind of business, I never questioned his love and respect for me. Consequently, we trusted each other at every level. It was a good partnership and, while it was definitely an intense lifestyle, for a decade we managed to become a leading provider of cell-site construction services throughout the West Coast. I had initiated a push into higher-value specialized technical services, project management, and land-use planning, and soon we were working on larger, more strategic projects.

In 1998, the cellular network industry was booming, and we considered selling our business. By the fall of that year, after several meetings with potential acquirers, we agreed to sell the business to a publicly traded competitor for up to $18 million in stock and cash. This was a very generous valuation of the business. We needed to achieve a full year of good results after the deal in order to earn-out the entire amount possible, so we developed a $1 million bonus plan to motivate our key leaders to achieve the goal and to share some of the fruits of victory. We barely made it, but we collected the entire amount. It seemed to me the many years of working with no salary at the commune had been adequately rewarded, and then some.

I wanted to be on the board of directors of the public company as a way to continue my professional growth and stay in the "inner ring" of how decisions would be made in the new company. My advisers laughed at my request, thinking it an overreach on my part. But, again, *I was not deterred*. At 27 years old, I found myself flying between Philadelphia and British Columbia, Canada serving as a director of a publicly traded company with a near-billionaire and handful of very accomplished business veterans. I had achieved status and financial success beyond what I could have possibly imagined back in the commune days.

I was now a confirmed multi-millionaire with the winds of success at my back. I was young, and I was ambitious.

CHAPTER 2
A Great Divide

It didn't take me long to buy a Porsche. I'd grown up with a picture of a red Carrera on my bedroom wall. It was one of those things I couldn't wait to possess. I hoped it would bring back that rush I felt as a boy when I imagined driving that car down a winding country road with leaves gently fluttering across the pavement as I blew by. I sent the money to the dealer, and they shipped me a bluish-purple convertible. I can still recall that smell of new leather and the trademark growl of the engine. We joined the country club, picked a lot in the nicest neighborhood in town, and built a lovely home in yuppie suburbia outside Portland, Oregon. Life was pretty good.

Selling that first business became a major milestone for my family. It marked the completion, in many ways, of our exodus from the commune. We were proud of our success, but also quite unprepared for it. My dad retired, but I went to work with the "NewCo" that acquired our business. I didn't have to move offices but was still adjusting to working inside a larger company where I didn't call the shots. At the same time, Helen and I were learning to live in the new normal, where money was no longer a constraint. Everything felt new and invigorating.

A GRAND EPIPHANY

As a 28-year-old Vice President of NewCo, I was thrown into a brave new world. I had gone from commune, to construction worker, to small business owner, to cog in the corporate wheel in fairly short order. One day I had a crystalizing epiphany on my way to the restroom. I was struck with the thought that all of humanity could effectively be divided into two groups: people who want to **get things done** and people who want to **stay out of trouble.**

Standing at the urinal, I can still visualize going through a Rolodex of associates, mentally tossing each to their rightful bucket. Of course, at that time, coming off a huge win, I formed moral judgments about both groups. The doers were what Ayn Rand might call the "producers;" noble, self-sacrificing, and brave because they have to break all the rules in order to get stuff done. People like me, or so I envisioned. And what about the folks who wanted to stay out of trouble? Well, they were mostly just scared, I thought, and in need of leadership and perhaps destined for a life of envy since they didn't have what it took to make things happen. These people would always be the necessary, slightly boring, middle class living a life dictated by circumstances around them. Listening now, you and I can easily hear a better-than-others arrogance paired with an oversized ego! That being said, over time I've observed more than a grain of truth in this cold dissection of humanity. Some people really *do* want to make things happen, and other people really *do* want to stay out of trouble.

"There are people who **want** to **get things done** and people who **want to stay out of trouble.**"

Not everyone has the same level of aspiration or interest in pioneering new ground. Virginia Postrel, in her book *The Future and Its Enemies*, puts forth an argument that divides people as stasists or dynamists. One is focused on maintaining stability. The other is all about change. "With some exceptions, the enemies of the future aim their attacks not at creativity itself but at the dynamic processes through which it is carried...All of these processes are shaping an unknown, and unknowable, future. Some people look at such diverse, decentralized choice-driven systems and rejoice, even when they don't like particular choices. Others recoil. In pursuit of stability and control, they seek to eliminate or curb these unruly or too-creative forces."

Dynamists look at the world around them, assess it realistically, and then seek to make improvements to better themselves, solve a problem, or just have some fun. Stasists, on the other hand, look at the way the world is and then position themselves to work within those constraints to find safety, stability, and recognition. Their power comes from the cards they were dealt, and they don't want anyone reshuffling the deck. Dynamists are willing to shuffle the deck and even change the game altogether in order to make something new happen.

A FOND FAREWELL

I wasn't long for NewCo. I was frustrated by a larger organization where the level of interaction with my supervisor was a weekly request from his executive assistant for my update. My inner voice shouted, "Why don't you answer my last update!?!" I observed that everyone likes to make deals, pop champagne, and talk about mergers and acquisitions, but post-merger integration of companies is actually a lot of hard work. I was tapped to assist in that project, but, frankly, didn't have a clue how to do it well. Given my background then, that should not have been a surprise.

I was already feeling restless as the corporate politics reared their head. As turf wars began, one of the leaders I brought with me was about to be fired for bogus reasons. I thought the divisional executive, who had taken his company public then bought our company, was afraid to confront and address these inequities. When I learned my friend was about to be fired, I picked up the phone and called the executive. He didn't answer, so I left a voicemail suggesting that if he was going to fire my friend he would need to fire me, too. I also took the opportunity to recommend he take some of the money he made in the sale of his own company and buy himself a set of testicles. This invitation to fire me was evidently an offer he couldn't refuse because I got my own voicemail a few days later letting me know I didn't need to come to work anymore. Probably not one of my smarter moves. At that point I had more money than brains and, evidently, felt compelled to prove it.

I was glad to be out from leadership I didn't respect. And I wasn't at all concerned with facing change.

THE DNA OF AMBITIOUS LEADERS

I've come to believe that entrepreneurs, mavericks, and innovators are all stimulated by the idea of change. You've probably noticed by now that I've lumped these types of people into what I call *ambitious* people. From time to time, I'll call them (us) other things, too: type-A, driven, hard-chargers, go-getters, leaders, determined, achievers, dynamists, and more. Chances are if you've picked up this book and made it to the second chapter, you've been described by one or all of these monikers as well. For simplicity, let's agree no one word encapsulates the nuances that describe humans who want to get things done and make a difference with their time. Since we chose *Ambition* as the title of the book, we'll roll with **ambitious** people for the most part.

Ambitious people are motivated by what others see as impossible, and fundamentally forward-focused. We're a lot less concerned about hanging on to what we have than we are about getting what's next. We have high aspirations and an action bias with an irrepressible tendency to ask why it's always been done that way. We assume there is a better way, or at least that there could be. We're the dreamers. That's not to say we have all the skills required to be successful. We don't. We have all the skills required to be dangerous. We have the ability to recruit others toward grand visions and projects, sometimes without a clue how to pull it all off.

Ambitious people tend to have a lot of energy and skills that give them influence over others. Speaking from my own experience, we often self-identify as leaders, and when a volunteer is needed or a question to the group is posed, it's our blood pressure that rises and our pulse that races. We know we'll be the one who takes the assignment. We know we'll be the one the group asks to lead the exercise. At some point, we stop resisting.

In high school, I recall being called into the principal's office to explain why we had the substitute art teacher in tears. As I tried to weasel out of any consequences, I pointed out that I couldn't possibly be the ringleader since I was an underclassman. Having none of it, the principal first reminded me that my dad was on the school board and then let me know that even though I was a lowly sophomore, I was still a leader. Funny how it takes someone else to tell you what you believe about yourself.

Fortunately, like we all have, I had people along the way who made a special effort to connect and encourage me. Having someone believe in and speak to your success has unbelievable power to draw us to our best selves.

Obviously, that affirmation of my leadership gift stuck with me—I'm writing about it 30 years later. Over the years, I committed to being a lifelong learner of how to become a good leader. Growing up inside a commune felt like a case study in leadership-gone-bad and created in me a desire to see leadership done well. In youth, I was a squirrelly trouble-maker, easily bored. As I matured, I realized being a leader is a gift and an obligation, and I purposed to become a good one. For me, that involves being intentional about almost every area of my life. It means remaining connected to people who bring out the best in me, people who inspire me. It also means developing the habits of good leaders, which we will explore later in the book.

Most people I know socially have no idea what I do professionally. They know I'm a business guy, somehow involved in technology. They certainly didn't think I was an author (maybe by now you don't either!). Having breakfast with a good friend at a local diner, the topic of this book came up. "What's it about?" he asked. "It's about how ambitious people struggle to find content-ment," I responded, offering my normal elevator pitch. "Well, content people struggle to find ambition, too," he quipped. The response dazed me. I guess I'd never really considered that reality. I don't know what that would feel like to struggle to find ambition. For me, and for most ambitious leaders, the world feels like a canvas of op-portunities and desires that, when pursued, give birth to tasks that have to be completed.

So, we're mostly anxious about accomplishing great things, and then we're anxious about all the tasks that need to get done to pull off what we started. Our natu-ral state is AAA—almost always anxious. It's interesting that anxiety and a sense of boredom can show up almost simultaneously. Hard-chargers get so accustomed to run-ning at a breakneck pace with the world at our command that the moment we're not entertained, challenged, or en-gaged by something deemed "important," we start feeling bored. In those moments, perhaps we could more honest-ly describe what we are feeling as restlessness: the feeling that we should be working or making progress with one of our many initiatives. Like maybe the world will pass us by if we take a little break.

Needless to say, someone else will have to write a book helping people find ambition.

That's not a problem I'm equipped to write about. Sure, I have down days and get wiped out by the flu like everybody else, but, for the most part, the struggle I face is the struggle to find a sense of contentment. I should be clear at this point in the book that contentment and satisfaction may be used interchangeably throughout. By content or satisfied I don't mean satisfied to the point we will never again pursue. Nor do I mean so content that we'll never again take on a new project. Otherwise, ambitious people wouldn't seek contentment at all! We like our work, and we like setting big, hairy, audacious goals that spark our sense of adventure. Content or satisfied means that we have ceased striving or are pleased with the results based on our expectation.

The process of understanding what motivates you will take time. One of the problems with ambitious leaders is that we are notoriously impatient. We have an action bias. I don't like this...let me *do* something. I don't feel fulfilled...let me *do* something. Then we're back in the fray, though not necessarily hitting any particular target because we never slowed down long enough to get clear on why we started a new initiative or what we were truly aiming for. Again, this process of understanding ourselves and our motivations takes time. There aren't shortcuts. The longer it takes you to begin intentionally seeking the answers to the question of what has been motivating you, the longer it will take you to make the adjustments that lead to contentment. We'll explore those motivations in Chapter 7.

For the record, I decided to sell the Porsche within a few years. After parking it, I was often drawn back for a long second glance. I wasn't quite sure whether I owned that car or it owned me. We said goodbye after a mere 7,000 miles. It was fun while it lasted, but I had developed a sense that this financial success wasn't helping my character. I had started to accumulate possessions, but they weren't really scratching the itch. I felt a growing identity crisis percolating beneath the surface. I was hungry for a sense of purpose and satisfaction that I wasn't finding...yet.

"For most **ambitious people,**
the **promise of peace** is a **mythical**
place rarely visited."

CHAPTER 3
Satisfaction and Expectations

Fire, when harnessed, warms and powers the world. But, when fire breaks from containment, property and lives are consumed and destroyed. Ambition is fire. When ambition lacks containment, many good-intentioned and talented leaders flame out, leaving in their wake a trail of broken trust and relationships. None of us wants to be that person, but left unmanaged, ambition turns hollow and destructive. Managed properly, however, ambition can be cultivated into a great strength; therefore, I attach no negative connotation to the word ambition. The leaders who make the biggest impact in the world are those who avoid getting burned by their own ambition.

For most ambitious people, the promise of peace is a mythical place rarely visited—let alone lived in. We nearly always struggle to find contentment. We may change the world while, at the same time, wrestling with a deep dissatisfaction that prevents us from enjoying the victory.

Coming off that first business sale, I felt the fire to do more. There was more to be done and accomplished and I was behind where I wanted to be. Consequently, I began investing in a variety of opportunities that came my way. Most of them blew up in my face and failed to produce the kind of financial or emotional rewards I was looking for. I was chasing the rainbow, often at the expense of my wife and kids. Work was easier for me than being fully engaged with family. On the surface, life was fine. But, underneath, there was anxiety and stress. Beautiful family, beautiful lifestyle, good friends, good church family, but I was unsettled.

I now consider myself a student of leadership and my own ambition. In my business career, I've had the privilege of co-founding, growing, and selling several multi-million dollar companies, serving either as a senior executive or chief executive. The intervening time between that first sale and the latest were intensely educational and, at times, painful. Bill Gates has said, "Success is a lousy teacher. It seduces smart people into thinking they can't lose."

If, as Gates suggests, success is a lousy teacher, does that imply our failures are a better teacher? While that may sound a bit demoralizing, I have found it to be true. I recall hearing a teacher on the radio suggest we really learn one of two ways: through wisdom (the experience of others) or through consequences. I was horrified to think about how much good advice I'd run past on my way to brick walls of my own choosing. We may want to call them "lessons learned" to make us feel a bit more affirmed, but we can agree that many ambitious leaders obtain wisdom through their mistakes. I don't mind sharing my mistakes with you, although I prefer to think of them as road signs along a winding country road informing the driver there is a bridge missing up ahead. If I know there's a bridge out, I feel an obligation to pass along that insight. In the end, you and I want to better understand how we can harness our ambition toward what matters most.

HOW HIGH WILL YOU SET YOUR HOPES?

Ambitious leaders, almost by definition, have high aspirations. One's aspiration level is the answer to the internal question of "How high will I set my hopes?" Like many personality characteristics, our level of aspiration is shaped both by our biological hardwiring (nature) and our environment (nurture).

Because I grew up in a commune, I partially understand that I was surrounded by an ethos of being different and doing things differently. Upon further reflection, I see now that there was a pervasive idea of being better than others and, therefore, needing to uphold the appearances of doing everything better than others. While that was a heavy (and arrogant) burden, I believe this mindset fueled a hyper-entrepreneurial spirit in many of the people who came and went though the commune. That certainly is true for my story. I also observe that Americans, in general, have historically held the belief that we can accomplish whatever we set our mind to, regardless of obstacles. While today's grievance-based cultural undertones risk creating simultaneous attitudes of entitlement and hopelessness, for the most part, the "American Dream" is still part of our psyche and vocabulary. We still believe we can have that house, that we can start that business, that we can send our kids to that school—if we're just willing to put in the work. This belief that we can achieve permeates the American experience, and I hope that never changes. However, we should be careful in how we set our expectations.

DISAPPOINTMENT IS TIED TO EXPECTATION

A lot of factors go into how high we set our hopes. In almost every area of life—what we look for in a spouse, how we envision family life, the type of income we expect, how fulfilling our sex life will be, how we perform with projects that intimidate us—whether we are mindful or not, we must acknowledge that we have aspirations. Think carefully about this next point. *Disappointment is tied to expectation.*

How we experience satisfaction is tied directly to the expectations we set for ourselves. The more thoughtful, open, and realistic we are with the expectations we set for ourselves, the higher our level of satisfaction can be. Stated simply, satisfaction is having our expectations met. Avoiding overfilling our calendar and learning how to say no to nonessential activities pays huge dividends in the form of margin to think, recreate, or connect with others. I'm not suggesting that we aim low. But I am admitting that we often construct unrealistic expectations for ourselves or allow others to construct expectations of us that cause us to become anxious, burdened, or disappointed when those expectations aren't met. I've also discovered that the expectations we provide to others are often a source of anxiety. When we take on responsibilities, we set internal and external expectations of how we would like to perform those duties. When we don't live up to those expectations we've formed for ourselves, we get anxious. This is when we are tempted to work even harder, get defensive, or even drink the pressures away.

"Stated simply, **satisfaction** is **having** our **expectations met.**"

This is a massive trap for ambitious leaders with the habit of starting projects and building things.

The higher our aspirations and the stronger our ambitions, the more frequent and profound our disappointments. Managing disappointments defines our level of maturity as a leader. We won't always get what we want. In fact, think about what that would be like if we actually *did* get everything we wanted *all the time*. Most of us would become unbearable tyrants! Learning to process the disappointments we encounter in healthy ways keeps us from becoming bitter and miserable to be around. Every time we start something new, we form new expectations, and it's those very expectations that determine our satisfaction with the eventual outcome. So, we need to do two things well: set good expectations and be prepared to handle disappointments. In baseball, a good batter strikes out twice for every hit. A venture capital model might count on one breakthrough success for every nine investment duds. Disappointment is a part of life that ambitious people must learn to wrestle with. We don't plan to fail, but we need a plan for when our expectations aren't met. One strategy is to give yourself permission to celebrate wins and to grieve losses, but not for very long. It's been suggested that 24 hours is sufficient for both, then it's back to work, leaving the past and focusing on what we can do today. In Chapter 6, we'll explore the role that gratitude can play in managing the powerful emotions ambitous people encounter.

Several years ago, I experienced one of the most painful professional losses of my life. I was serving as the president of a company that sold equipment to improve cellular coverage inside large venues such as stadiums, airports, subways, etc. I grew up in a state without a professional football team, so I adopted the San Francisco 49ers as my team. As luck would have it, the 49ers were building a new stadium just seven minutes from our corporate offices in the Bay Area. The stadium would be a showcase for new technology in the heart of the Silicon Valley, and we were invited to provide a bid on the project. I could see it...maybe even taste it. I toured the mock-up hospitality suites at the 49ers' sales office. We visited representatives of the team to build rapport. I visited the old Candlestick Park to meet key decision makers. Our team labored for weeks to reinvent our entire proposal response package to be the best we'd ever been. We were all in. Then I screwed it up...and we lost the deal. I led my team down a bad path with a flawed pricing strategy and we got clocked. After we presented to the decision makers, we debriefed over lunch at a nearby suburban restaurant. It occurred to us that the potential customer hadn't asked us a single question in the presentation. I assumed it was because our proposal fit their needs so perfectly. A vice president who joined us pointed out that perhaps they'd already made up their mind. I still recall standing at one of our industry's biggest trade shows a few weeks later when we got the news that the project was being awarded to an upstart competitor. My stomach dropped...I was in denial. How could this be?

I had become so overly invested in the vision I had for this one particular project that I *felt* as though my entire professional life (and let's face it, personal life) was a failure. I imagined everyone in my industry talking about how we lost this deal, or, even worse, saying good things about the competitor who outplayed us. It was overwhelming disappointment like I hadn't experienced before.

Suffice it to say, I did not handle the loss with grace. In fact, I spent every waking moment for the next few weeks trying to blow up the deal for our competitor. Asking questions about process, calling in favors, casting doubts…but, in the end, I simply lost. And the more I thought about it, the more I realized that I had let my expectations grow beyond a safe, rational level. Gradually, I became embarrassed about the way I handled the loss and had to pick up the phone and place apology calls for my behavior. Fortunately, I found understanding from the recipients of those calls. In fact, I remember one leader telling me, "No need to apologize, you're a competitive guy." True, but I also acted like an entitled brat and had violated my own conscience. In the end, my company had plenty of high-profile wins to celebrate, and I learned not to get too attached to any project, no matter how special. Disappointment is tied to expectation. Did I mention I'm now a Seahawks fan?

THE WISDOM OF COUNSELORS

One of the best ways that ambitious leaders can manage the downside of the expectation trap is to intentionally develop relationships with wise counselors who understand their gifts, passions, and capabilities. To go even further, when those counselors can encourage you toward your calling and purpose, things get really good.

"**Disappointment** is tied
to **expectation**."

The more we know, the more we (should) realize what we don't know. Leading up to the sale of my last company, I began handing off the leadership reins to my executive vice president who was being promoted to president. I took the time to point out all of the people I had surrounded myself with in order to help guide my decisions. I went through a partial list and even surprised myself with the amount of support I had gathered: a board of shareholders, a management consulting firm including a seasoned mentor, a forum of seven other CEOs with whom I met monthly, a personal leadership coach, a top-notch lawyer, a savvy CPA, and a long list of executive peers. The point wasn't to show him how connected I was (although I did take pleasure in that!), but, instead, to point out how much, as a leader, I needed input from people who could provide the guardrails and guidance to my role as the visionary. One of the best ways to keep your expectations appropriately sized is developing a trusted team around you to bounce dreams and schemes off of. To be a successful leader, we have to develop the tools to process disappointments in a healthy way. I'm convinced a lot of addictions stem from processing disappointment (experienced as hurt) with drugs, alcohol, pornography, food, relationships, etc. We have to face the facts — as ambitious leaders wanting to make a difference in this world, we're going to be disappointed often. If we weren't regularly disappointed, we wouldn't be aiming high enough for our own standards.

CHAPTER 4
Entrepreneurs in Danger

TWO SIDES OF A COIN

During an extremely difficult season of life when everything that I touched turned to dross instead of gold, I reached out to my friend, Dave, for support. I had met Dave when he was serving as a pastor in Portland, Oregon, but I didn't meet him at a church. The day following the 9/11 terrorist attacks, the small investment banking firm I was working at asked Dave to speak to the employees of the firm. I immediately was struck with the bravery of this guy—only in his 30s—standing in front of people he didn't know talking about how to make sense of something so senseless. He handled the assignment with a deft touch, and eventually we began attending his church. I got to know his story over a round of poorly-played golf. Best I could tell, Dave had always been an overachiever. He was headed for the Naval Academy to fly jets but took a detour to become a mechanical engineer. After a few years as an engineer for Chevrolet, he felt a call to ministry and moved to Dallas for theological training. From there, he was launched into a pastorate near Portland. (Yes, his wife was a *very* patient woman.) But Dave is the kind of guy worth betting on. His sermons were deep and relevant, reflecting the mind of someone who was curious about everything.

After several years of trying to get the fledgling church off the ground, Dave eventually left the ministry, heading back to the East Coast to lick his wounds and regroup with his small family. Not one to wallow in indecision, Dave decided to go to medical school. I liked Dave a lot, and we kept in touch sporadically. During this particularly tough season in my business and family life, I called Dave to get some perspective and emotional support. I felt caught in a cycle of failure. Nothing was working, but I felt determined to keep grinding. Somewhere in the conversation, the topic of ambition came up and Dave shared a lesson he had learned that rocked my core. "When I was in seminary, Dr. Hendricks taught us that every positive character trait has a corresponding negative trait on another side of the coin," he said. I encouraged him to go on. "If we take ambition, for instance, the other side of that very same coin is often envy." Arghh. I was busted. I always knew that I had a hard time rooting for the success of others, but I had never really heard it so bluntly. In many ways, I had been driven by envy of what others possessed or had accomplished. Most people don't mind being called ambitious, but no one wants to be called envious. To this day, that simple conversation continues to remind me to question my underlying motivation, especially when I am flushed with emotions such as anxiety, jealousy, or impatience.

"**Most people don't mind** being **called ambitious**, but **no one wants** to be called **envious**."

THE SPIRIT OF THE ENTREPRENEUR

Whether hidden in the cloistered halls of academia and religion, in the discipline of medicine and law, or the rough and tumble worlds of business and politics, we observe certain personalities not satisfied with the status quo. These mavericks, hard-chargers, and innovators thrive on solving problems. If there is no problem to solve, they'll create one just to feel like they're making progress. One of my favorite historical figures is Teddy Roosevelt. He was an over-the-top overachiever who threw himself into grand projects across an immense spectrum of life. He was an American statesman, author, explorer, war hero, naturalist, and reformer who served as governor of New York and the 26th President of the United States from 1901 to 1909.[ii]

"In a lifetime of remarkable achievement, Roosevelt had shaped his own character—and that of his country—through sheer force of will, relentlessly choosing action over inaction, and championing what he famously termed *the strenuous life*. From his earliest days of childhood, that energetic credo had served as his compass and his salvation, propelling him to the forefront of public life, and lifting him above a succession of personal tragedies and disappointments. Each time he encountered an obstacle, he responded with more vigor, more energy, more raw determination."

Webster defines the word *entrepreneur* as: one who organizes, manages, and takes on the risks of a business or enterprise. Since the entrepreneurial spirit and personality type weaves across career types, I don't think entrepreneurs are constrained merely to the world of business. While entrepreneurs are often imagined as the Silicon Valley whiz kids who build billion-dollar businesses that change society, being an entrepreneur is much less about what one does than about how one thinks and takes action upon those thoughts.

AVOIDING PITFALLS

Entrepreneurs are my tribe. They are some of my favorite people since I easily relate to what makes them tick. I've noticed that in today's celebrity-driven culture we celebrate entrepreneurs while overlooking the common pitfalls they will certainly face. That's the equivalent of looking at a balance sheet and choosing only to see the assets, never the liabilities. Using the two-sided coin observation I picked up from my pal, Dave (M.D.!), I've spent significant time pondering the upside and downside of several characteristics common to entrepreneurs while reflecting on how these traits show up in my own experiences.

ENTREPRENEURS ARE **DETERMINED.**

- The positive side of being determined is that we will stick with the plan against all odds. We'll show up early, we'll double down on the venture we started. We'll do whatever it takes because our pain threshold is higher than average.

- The negative side of being determined is that we will stick with the plan against all *evidence*! Some might even call this being stubborn.

I knew I was guilty of being "stubborn" during one of the most expensive lessons, which came from starting several franchise restaurants. My grand vision was to form the venture, fund a management team, then go to the mailbox and collect profit checks. Sounds simple, right? Unfortunately, I made a variety of strategic blunders. Starting too many locations before I knew how to operate them, picking bad locations...the list goes on. After years of grinding away, I found myself being pulled into the operations of the actual restaurants to try to get them working. It was humbling going from a board room to delivering pizzas. True, I owned the pizza company, but, nevertheless, I knew my plan wasn't working. I brought in an expert to look at our operations, and I'll never forget his comment. He looked at how much money we had lost and how long we'd been doing it and he said, "I'm always amazed there are people like you." Whereas I had the temperament and bankroll to keep slogging, he would have pulled the plug long before.

One night while laying in bed, Helen and I had a heart to heart about our restaurant venture. "I'm willing to be the martyr here," I told her. "But I have no confidence I can fix this." Then I blurted the summary of our current reality: "I'm really bad at running restaurants, we're losing our butt...and I hate it." Her response reminds me of why it's so very important to marry well. She said, "You need to do something you love." She could have busted my chops for wasting her retirement funds or not being able to remodel the house like she wanted (and I promised). She never did. The following week we began shutting down the restaurants, making a commitment to pay back the lenders. Somebody a little less determined might have done that years before and skipped the painful "lessons."

ENTREPRENEURS ARE **BOLD.**

- The positive side of being bold is that we are willing to go where no man has gone before. We're the explorers and the pioneers.

- The negative side of being bold is that we are often reckless, operating by our gut and emotion rather than insight and careful consideration. The adage "fools rush in" comes to mind.

One of the franchises I started was a premium ice cream shop. Somehow I thought it would be a good idea to open up the business in the same small town that boasts one of the West Coast's most award-winning ice cream producers. Of course, people loved our product, but we soon discovered when our rural demographic could buy something of comparable quality at a third of the price just a few blocks away, they did. Shocking, I know!

ENTREPRENEURS ARE **GOAL ORIENTED.**

- The positive side of being goal oriented is that we set our mind on an outcome, break it down into bite-sized chunks, and get after it. We're hard-chargers.

- The negative side of being goal oriented is that we often lack patience and empathy for people who aren't.

I once participated in a conference call with a leader who specialized in helping leaders shift from "success to significance." He explained the disharmony leaders often experience when shifting from the corporate world to going full-time in a non-profit. He said business leaders often show up in this new world and "blow all the fuses." We might ride in on a white horse full of wisdom and clarity without taking the time to understand the culture or history of the very organizations we're trying to help. Years later, I remember trying to provide some "structure" to an executive at an organization where I served on the board. After some grinding of the gears, the executive confessed that he felt like I was drowning him with tasks. I was baffled because it felt like I was stuck in first gear and the executive just wasn't getting it. I was used to working with type-A leaders in the commercial world, and he was in a different solar system altogether. I've often thought about what I could have done differently to build trust or empathy with this particular leader, if for no other reason than to avoid some of the frustration and hurt feelings that surfaced.

ENTREPRENEURS HAVE A **HIGH REJECTION TOLERANCE.**

- The positive side of a high rejection tolerance is that we simply won't take *no* for an answer. I think of politicians like Abraham Lincoln who faced public defeat so many times before finding his place in history.

- The negative side of high rejection tolerance is that we can easily become entitled, thinking we deserve a *yes*.

I shared the story of my 49ers loss earlier. It startled me how entitled I had become with this one opportunity. Particularly because I have a personal pet peeve with people who behave as though they are entitled. They keep a long list of all the sacrifices they've made in the past, and then dump them on the table when they request whatever they're now demanding. Few personality types cause me so much frustration. I once joined a webinar on how to keep our kids from becoming entitled monsters and heard a great summary of the entitlement mindset: Entitled people think they deserve *special treatment*. Looking at that definition helped me realize I'm often acting more entitled than I'd care to admit.

ENTREPRENEURS ARE **GENERALLY RULES-AVERSE.**

- The positive side of being rules-averse is that we're willing to think beyond the perceived constraints that hold others back. Rules are guidelines for sta-sists who need the structure. We're dynamists, darn it, let us show you how to get this done even if we have to color outside the traditional (not moral) lines a bit.

- The negative side of being rules-averse is that we are too often willing to override prudent advice. Earlier I mentioned that we either learn from the wisdom of others or through consequences. Often, in our desire to move quickly or our belief that rules were made for others, we're unwilling to consider that there are principles in place that will affect us, whether we ignore them or not.

Unfortunately, hindsight is hauntingly clear. I can remember being at a charity event on a beautiful hillside in Oregon where I was talking with a local business leader about my plan to open some franchise restaurants. He warned me, "One of the problems with franchises is that there's almost no equity value in the business." I took a mental note, but I took no action. Even if his "opinion" was true, surely I could find a way around that truth. Furthermore, my plan was already in motion. Years later, after trying unsuccessfully to sell the restaurants, that conversation came back to me with amazing clarity as I was selling equipment for pennies on the dollar.

ENTREPRENEURS ARE **INDEPENDENT.**

- The positive side of being independent is that we can figure out how to get things done without a lot of involvement from others.

- The negative side of being independent is that we often don't ask good questions or consult with our legal, tax, business advisers, or mentors before it's too late.

I recall making a massive investment in (yet another) friend's new business before the business was really off the ground. I'd already wired the money and let the situation crumble before I ever spoke about it with my lawyer. Had I spoken with her, we would have certainly tied the investment into deliverables from the company, making sure the plan unfolded as planned before my full investment was at risk. Operating independently had cost me a small fortune.

ENTREPRENEURS ARE **CURIOUS.**

- The positive side of being curious is that we are often, as Jim Collins describes in his classic book, *Good to Great*, like a fox: quick minded and worldy. We're interested in a thousand things and love the process of discovery.

- The negative side of being curious is that we are often so focused on exploring new ideas that we don't focus on building the people or systems necessary for the type of long term impact we desire. We don't, as Collin suggests, operate like a hedgehog, who is able to focus on that one thing hedgehogs do—dig hedgehog holes. Innovation + Consistency = Progress. Without consistency, we spin circles chasing pipe dreams.

ENTREPRENEURS ARE **UNDER-RESOURCED.**

- The positive side of being under-resourced is that we are forced into Wile E. Coyote levels of ingenuity. In order to get things done, we learn how to create solutions with little more than baling wire and duct tape until the revenue starts to flow and we can hire people and buy what we need to make the business work.

- The negative side of being under-resourced is that we often lack the horsepower and leverage to achieve our goals. Our dreams can die because we don't have the human and financial capital to pull them off.

I believe stereotyping entrepreneurism with the idea of a small, independent, under-resourced business starting in a garage is a mistake. Coming from where I did, this was my original conception of what an entrepreneur looked like. Over time, I discovered that the entrepreneurial spirit can accomplish great things inside larger, well-capitalized organizations whether military, business, or even academia...*if* the entrepreneur can tolerate the structured environment that often evolves as an organization grows.

ENTREPRENEURS WITH RESOURCES ARE **DANGEROUS.**

"Give me a lever long enough and a fulcrum on which to place it, and I shall move the world."
— Archimedes

AND, FINALLY, ENTREPRENEURS ARE **AMBITIOUS.**

- The positive side of being ambitious is that we are energetic, forward thinkers. We take initiative and create motion toward something that doesn't yet exist.

Saying entrepreneurs and leaders are ambitious is a little bit like saying water is wet, but here we arrive again at the central idea of this book:

- The negative side of being ambitious is that we commonly carry a deep sense of dissatisfaction with the way things are *now*. We are often ungrateful for what we already have, regardless of how good we have it.

This insight is loaded with the potential to dramatically change the way you live and lead. The natural state of the ambitious leader is not gratitude. It's closer to dissatisfaction. There is always a problem to solve, a mountain to climb, or a process to improve. If we want to live in a place of gratitude, we are going to have to work at it.

CHAPTER 5
Chasing Cars

Golfers say there are two things in life that don't last: pros that make pars and dogs that chase cars.

As Americans, we live in a society pushing us to achieve and excel. We are driven to accomplish, win, and succeed. Ostensibly for the purpose of building wealth to provide the "economic security" we need for ourselves and our dependents. Ambitious people optimize their entire life for chasing their goal, developing habits and mental muscles tied to execution of their work. Whether building a business, pursuing a Ph.D., or hitting "the number" financially, many of us have no plan for what happens *after* we achieve our goal. We're the proverbial dog chasing the car, unsure of what happens when we sink our teeth into the tire.

When someone sells a business, inherits money, or achieves a major monetary breakthrough, there are many new financial, psychological, and cultural challenges ahead. The more immature we are at the time we find economic success, the more likely we will learn these lessons the hard way.

SUDDEN WEALTH SYNDROME

My financial story would be a lot different if I had taken money from the sale of my first company and parked it in tax-free municipal bonds. At least, until such time, I had a plan. I felt certain that since I was able to generate so much success in my 20s, there was even more success to be had, and that I needed to get after it right away. I was suffering from Sudden Wealth Syndrome, and I didn't even know it.

I first learned the phrase Sudden Wealth Syndrome in an article featuring a dot-com millionaire who had struck it rich. By this time, I was already the dog that caught the car tire, and I was in the middle of the thump, thump, thump of learning things the hard way. I remember just one quote from the article: "Having more money just allowed me to make bigger mistakes."

There's an old adage that says, "A fool and his money are soon parted." I added a second part based on observation to this classic: "But no one wants to hear him cry about it." Trust me, I don't enjoy rehashing mistakes, but I do enjoy seeing people learn from them. I'm grateful to have these insights to draw from at this stage of life.

Sudden Wealth Syndrome expert Stephen Goldbart and his associates at the Money, Meaning & Choices Institute say that much like the four stages of grief, there are four stages people go through when coming to terms with their new wealth:

Honeymoon: Like the honeymoon phase of a love relationship, people who first come into money feel powerful and invulnerable. Many go on spending sprees, buying things and making risky investments (often with disastrous results).

Wealth Acceptance: In this stage, the view of oneself as powerful and invincible is mixed with a sense of vulnerability and the realization for the need to set limits.

Identity Consolidation: During this stage, people accept that they are monetarily wealthy, but realize that their money doesn't define them. They begin asking: "Who do I want to be?"

Stewardship: In this phase, people have reached a mature resolution of what their money means to them and have a plan for what to do with it in terms of a personal, familial, and philanthropic mission.[iii]

I sold my first business at 27, so when I look back on these four stages of managing new wealth, I can see that I barely made it through the honeymoon stage before I'd lost most of the value of what I'd earned in the sale. Though I shared the story about the Porsche, the truth is Helen and I were not conspicuous consumers who lived a lavish lifestyle. 1998 was a great time to sell a business, but it was a terrible time to make investments as we were turning toward a massive stock market meltdown that affected nearly every sector of the economy. But I felt like I needed to "get back in the game" and fancied myself an investor. In retrospect, I see that I didn't have clarity on what I was trying to accomplish, or, at the core, even *who* I was. Sort of a mini identity crisis.

I recall being at a men's retreat in Vail, Colorado when I had to step out from dinner to take a phone call. On the call I learned I'd just lost *yet another* chunk of money in a bad investment, this time in a friend's business. The next morning I vividly recall sharing with a few of the guys that my identity had always been the young, successful guy in every room. Now I was just young. Could I handle that?

In Robert Kiyosaki's classic book, *Cashflow Quadrant*, he teaches that there are four ways to approach work and wealth. One is to be an Employee working for others. Another is to be Self-employed, where you still have to show up and work. A third would be to own a Business where other people work for you (whether you show up or not). And, finally, to be an Investor, where instead of people working for you, your money works for you whether you get out of bed or not. He calls each of these a quadrant and labels them **E-S-B-I.** It's a great read before jumping into a major career move. But, by the time I read the book, I was already going 100 mph fancying myself an investor...which made the following paragraph all the more memorable. Memorable like a slap across the face.

"A quick word of caution. The "B" (Business) quadrant is much different than the "I" (Investor) quadrant. I've seen many successful business owners sell their businesses for millions, and their newfound wealth goes to their head. They tend to think that their dollars are a measure of their IQ, so they swagger on down to the "I" quadrant and lose it all. The game and rules are different in all of the quadrants...which is why I recommend education over ego."

MANAGING THROUGH MAJOR TRANSITION

Ambitious people set big goals. When a goal is achieved, there can be a massive vacuum. Something we liked a lot, maybe even loved, has been lost. It may have been exchanged for money (if you sold a business), but, truth be told, many of us aren't really in it for the money. We chase the dream because we like chasing the dream. We like the thrill and the freedom. We like having a high profile, perhaps being recognized by our peers and feeling like what we do is important. When a chapter in our life ends or we achieve a goal, even if it's a happy ending (goal achieved, cash in the bank, etc.), there is a visceral, sometimes drastic, letdown. This can be a danger zone for many ambitious people. William Bridges, in his book *Transitions: Making Sense of Life's Changes*, lays out some of the psychology associated with making a major transition.

"A transition is not simply a change. A change is a modification of your external situation. Its meaning is clear. You go on a diet and lose weight. You leave one job and take another. You pack your belongings and move to a new city. You get married.

"In contrast, a transition is an internal reorientation. It is primarily psychological in nature, and it requires adapting emotionally to new circumstances. Its nature and boundaries are not obvious. Transitions usually involve painful, blind groping from a settled phase of life to a new, unknown, and even threatening situation. They require you to give up old, comfortable ways of doing things or interpreting experiences and to find entirely new ones.

"Today, constant change is a fact of life. People easily manage to move to a new job or home, or even a new relationship or lifestyle. But they get into trouble during life's transitional periods. They may not even recognize what is happening to them. All they know is everything suddenly seems 'up in the air,' an experience that can be deeply unsettling. Transitions always include a disconcerting sense of 'in-betweenness.' They are difficult and painful, and they proceed in three stages, which you experience in an order that may seem backwards: the end, the neutral zone, and the new beginning."

The more we prepare ourselves for what happens after achievement, the better we will be able to foresee the emotions that come. Successfully making a transition from being a CEO of a tech company to being an unemployed writer (for a season) has taken some effort. My old identity is fading. I'm in the neutral zone headed toward a new beginning. There is always a temptation to go back to where, like an episode of Cheers, "Everybody knows your name." However, having talked through this transition with friends and mentors, I'm convinced that my writing, speaking, and coaching are aligned with my own purpose.

Similarly, not only does a transition create enormous stress on the individual going through it, the ripples affect those around them. Sudden financial success creates a new set of dynamics in family relations. Listening to the horror stories of lottery winners or watching family members come out of nowhere to fight over the assets of the deceased should be proof enough. Planning for success and the transitions it brings is a sign of maturity and thoughtfulness on our part.

AFFLUENZA

There's another reason many of us feel dissatisfied despite our relative prosperity: When affluent people become sick from their excess or the pursuit of even more affluence, they've contracted affluenza.

Statistically, most Americans are at the pinnacle of the most prosperous and healthy people groups in *history*. We hear a lot of political rhetoric about the 1 percent who run roughshod over the common people while they lobby and rig the game for their own benefit. Affluenza conjures up images of polo fields and yachts, or perhaps Gordon Gekko from the 1987 film, *Wall Street,* who famously offered, "Greed…is good. Greed is right. Greed works." Played by Michael Douglas, Gekko is a wealthy but ruthless corporate raider who brings the young stockbroker Bud Fox under his spell. In Gekko's valuing of money above people and relationships, the film sought to expose the greed and excess of the 1980s.

But a strange thing happened…Gekko became a bit of a folk hero/role model looked upon favorably as some young people chose careers on Wall Street as stockbrokers because of those characters in the movie. Not likely the intended consequence when Oliver Stone was writing the script, but also not surprising considering the messages we send our young people about the definitions of success.

The site, www.globalrichlist.com, invites us toward a reality check. "Didn't make it onto the yearly roll call of the mega-wealthy? Now's your chance to find out where you actually sit in comparison to the rest of the world." But punch in your income or assets and you'll learn just how far your funds would go in a developing country and just how far up the socioeconomic ladder you really are. We have better access to healthcare, education, housing, food, and economic security than at any other point in history. What if you and I and our entire peer group are revealed as part of this global 1 percent? How would this change our feelings about this 1 percent we hear so much about? Would we still want more?

How much is enough, anyway? Many of us leave that underlying question unasked—acting on general social norms related to wealth instead of finding an answer that fits our lives and our values. When John D. Rockefeller was asked, "How much would be enough?" he famously answered, "Just a little bit more." What an ironic answer, coming from America's wealthiest businessman who at the height of his financial success personally accounted for almost 2 percent of the total U.S. GDP!

But, regardless of income or wealth, the fact is we are conditioned by society to answer the question of, "How much is enough?" with an answer of "more."

We often begin conversations about finances from a place of scarcity and fear, a focus on worst-case scenarios, and a basis of comparative financial goals that views becoming wealthy (whatever that means personally) as the target.

How can it be that we are so fortunate, yet so unhappy with our lot? I believe the answer, to a large degree, is because we allow ourselves to be immersed with media images of those who have even more. We are poisoned by comparison.

The most pernicious and embarrassing reality of comparison is that we almost always compare ourselves with those who have more, not less.

Madison Avenue, the historical marketing epicenter in New York City, exists by pushing our buttons and creating a perpetual state of discontent. Though we're literally bombarded with these messages selling us "happiness," the actual value system we are constructing leads to a lack of fulfillment.

Dr. Tim Kasser is a professor of psychology at Knox College. Over the last decade, he has been especially focused on studying *materialistic values* (i.e., being wealthy, having many possessions, being attractive, and being popular). He contends that:

Despite the claims of consumer culture to the contrary, what research has shown in literally dozens of studies is that the more that people prioritize materialistic values, the less happy they are, the less satisfied they are with their lives, the less vital and energetic they feel, the less likely they are to experience pleasant emotions like happiness and **contentment** and joy, the more depressed they are, the more anxious they are, the more they experience unpleasant emotions like fear and anger and sadness, [and] the more likely they are to engage in the use of substances like cigarettes and alcohol.

"We are **poisoned**
by **comparison**."

We get up close and personal tours of celebrity homes, gourmet cooking, and daily insight into the rarified lifestyles of the super rich. Affluenza is showing its symptoms, and ambitious people are particularly susceptible to this social disease because they are, by nature, both capable and determined. While many people see what they want and conclude it's beyond their reach, ambitious people calculate differently. Ambitious people know they can find a way to get what they want if they are willing to pay the price. That's how we're wired, and, in America, there's not a lot holding us back.

Once, I was flying into Southern California and decided to see if I could connect with some great friends, the "Smiths." The Smiths are always a lot of fun, even though they're serious about their causes, their friends, and their business. They're the kind of people who exude excellence in whatever they do. And they lived in the most beautiful home I'd ever seen. When it came time to build a new home, they "replaced" a house in an exclusive, gated neighborhood and spared no expense to create a stunning home overlooking a manicured park and the Pacific. My family has enjoyed their legendary hospitality as house guests over the years.

Since I had given the Smiths limited notice on my arrival, I was invited to join them at a fundraiser they'd already committed to for the evening. Just being with the Smiths was always an adventure, even if not at their fine home.

Driving down beautiful California Highway 1, I was provided the location of the meetup. I parked my rental car and jumped in with the Smiths as we proceeded through a guarded gate, back over the highway, up and out to the edge of Emerald Point, where homes overlook the pristine Emerald Bay. It was rarified air, to be sure. We parked and made our way into the home where the fundraiser was to be held. Greeted by the hostess, we were ushered through a grand entrance into a world-class home unlike any I'd entered before. The expansive, panoramic views captured the most beautiful blue-green Pacific Ocean bay you can imagine.

Almost immediately, I was aware that the Smiths had invited me to a home that, to my total surprise, seemed to be built on an even grander scale than their own. Every luxury home deserves a fish tank, but this home had a fish tank that seemed to form the entire wall of the room. A walk-in closet is wonderful. This home had an exquisite marbled closet bigger than most country club locker rooms. I was seeing firsthand the reality that no matter what we build or possess in this life, someone will always have more, and if not more, at least a little better or different. If having the most or best is our source of happiness, we won't stay happy very long.

Recalling these California coast homes reminds me of an experience I had many years ago before I made a decision to move back to rural Oregon. I had been to a Christmas party at an associate's home high up in the hills of suburbia. The home had great views, a beautiful pool, two large curved staircases in the grand entry...and more. After the party, when I pulled into my own neighborhood and parked in the garage of my own "luxury" home, somehow, everything just seemed...smaller. The thought made me sick—not having an "under-sized" house, but how quickly I was losing appreciation for something that was well beyond my reach just a few years prior.

When affluenza has taken root, the primary identifying symptom is an unsatisfied appetite for more. Thousand-aires know a few millionaires, and envision themselves breaking into the ranks. Millionaires know some hun-dred-millionaires and imagine how much more is possi-ble when you add a few zeros to one's net worth. Hun-dred-millionaires compare private jets and occasionally get to mingle with billionaires from whom they can get advice on how to pick a good island or the merits of buy-ing a professional sports team. There will always be more than we have now.

> "Death and Destruction are never satisfied,
> and neither are human eyes."
> —Ancient literature

> "Comparison is the thief of joy."
> —Teddy Roosevelt

CHAPTER 6
Gratitude Adjustment

The central goal of this book is to answer the question of why ambitious people struggle to find satisfaction. There are two main reasons I believe this condition exists:

First, ambitious people are forward-focused and less likely to reflect on the past or even the present.

Second, ambitious people tend to believe that the path to satisfaction is achievement.

But I contend that satisfaction does not live on the other side of achievement. It lives on the other side of gratitude.

If we want to discover and remain in a lifestyle of satisfaction, we have to discover how to become grateful. Some of my least satisfied times came when I had the most material possessions. Why? Because joy is linked to gratitude, not possessions or achievement.

During one of the darkest and most painful seasons of my life, when our business, our marriage, and everything else seemed to be struggling, I was having heartfelt conversations with God about what was going wrong with my life. Was I being punished? Were my best days behind me? I could certainly recount plenty of mistakes and failures that might justify being in life's penalty box. It was during this time that I came to a clear self-assessment; I was ungrateful. I hadn't valued what I'd been given and

"But I contend that **satisfaction does not live on the other side of achievement. It lives on** the other **side of gratitude.**"

had been so focused on doing and earning more that I had not bothered to value and protect all the blessings I already had. In all truth, losing money was less painful than the loss of self-respect I was feeling. Fortunately, I believed both could be regained, but not without a serious adjustment to the way I lived my life—a gratitude adjustment.

For nearly a decade, I have pondered the idea of gratitude. Imagine carrying around a piece of paper with a single word on it for 10 years. That paper would become soft and tattered, but you'd take on a relationship with that word because you'd be forced to think of it every day. Your ear would become trained to hear synonyms or to catch the word in whispers of other people's stories and conversations. A writer once described the idea of writing as flypaper. Once you've identified the idea and started writing, you've hung the flypaper, and now related ideas, anecdotes, and evidence naturally start sticking to the flypaper. That's how I experience the idea of gratitude these days. I see it everywhere.

What is gratitude? We can conceptualize gratitude as a habit, a personality trait, a reaction, or even an emotion. For purposes of this book, we can define gratitude as "appreciation for something received." We'll keep it short and sweet.

There are myriad techniques people use to practice gratitude. I'll provide several here, but you'll need to be intentional about developing your own gratitude practice. If you're convinced that you struggle with feeling grateful, this chapter will be very helpful. If you've nearly always felt like you "can't get no satisfaction," I must tell you flatly: you never will without a gratitude adjustment.

A Morning Ritual: Many people start their day with some form of meditation and quiet time. Before email, before breakfast, before checking the news on their mobile device, they practice orienting their mind and heart toward what's most important. During this time, which often includes good reading material and goal review, they will identify and *express* thanks for several big and little things in their life. A *big* thing might be the companionship of their spouse and good health. A *small* thing might be the benefit of running water or the effort their child put into a science project. The power is in the recognition of a benefit received and the expression of thanks.

A Gratitude Journal: A simple search for "gratitude journal" on Amazon will yield a variety of products purpose-built to help you write out the things in your life that you are thankful for. Perhaps you feel like you'll run out of ideas. Just try it. "When you train the brain to become grateful for people, things, and experiences, the pieces of gratitude keep flowing like a bountiful river." –Russ Terry, author of *My Gratitude Journal.*

Service: Every Thanksgiving, many families across the U.S. find a way to serve at a rescue mission, food bank, or other social service institution. I think this is a great idea for exposure to the reality of those in our own communities who are in deep need. That being said, I don't believe coming into contact with those needs once

"We need **regular doses of reality** and **service** to **break through the insulations** of **comfort that grow around us.**"

a year will have much of an effect on us. We need regular doses of reality and service to break through the insulations of comfort that grow around us. Finding ways to become a servant, or a servant leader, is critical to growing in gratitude.

Recognition: I met a restaurant manager once who shared a technique he used to make sure he was being generous with positive feedback to his staff. He carried 10 dimes in his right pocket. Every time he provided positive feedback or recognition to one of his workers, he was allowed to move one dime from his right pocket to his left. His goal was to move all his dimes over by the end of the day. This was good management, but it was also good gratitude.

Expressing Thanks: *The Wall Street Journal* ran a brilliant article by Diana Kapp entitled, "Raising Children with an Attitude of Gratitude." I recommend you read the whole thing, but offer an appropriate excerpt here:

At the Branstens' modern white dining table, the family holds hands for their nightly ritual. Arielle, 8 years old, says she's thankful for her late grandfather, Horace, and how funny he was. "I'm missing him," she says. Her third-grade pal, over for dinner, chimes in, "I'm grateful for the sausages." Leela, who works for an education non-profit, and her attorney husband, Peter, burst into smiles. The San Francisco couple couldn't have scripted this better. Appreciation for things big and small—that's why the family does this. The simple question of, "What are you grateful for today?" has a powerful reorienting effect that changes the whole dynamic around the dinner table.*

Dave Kerpen, CEO of Likeable Local, says, "The main reason I handwrite three thank you cards every day is that it allows me to focus on others and transforms my mood from bad to good, from good to great, or from great to ecstatic. You can't be upset and grateful at the same time, and this practice puts me in a great mood—to have a great day—every single day."

MY OWN GRATITUDE ADJUSTMENT PRACTICE

I have my own gratitude adjustment exercise that keeps me balanced. There have been times where I've practiced it almost daily. In other seasons of life, I might go weeks without. If I'm doing it daily, I'm being proactive. If it's been a few weeks, the likelihood is that I'm becoming stressed and anxious, and I'll be reminded that without gratitude, *this* is what always happens to me. I'm ambitious, after all.

I don't think it would be fair for me to write a book that orbits the idea of gratitude without explaining a bit more about my own gratitude practice. I offer this not as a template, but as insight into what works for me. So... for me, shower time, like an airplane trip, is one of those rare moments where I'm isolated from conversation and expectations from others. I take that time to be honest about how I am feeling. If I am anxious, frustrated, impatient, stressed, or angry I know I am in a personal danger zone where I must take evasive, intentional action in a different direction. Here's what I do: First, because I am someone who values my relationship with God, I envision Him as a loving Father. Next, I think about all that He's done for me. And, finally, I think about all of the gifts and responsibilities I have been entrusted with. As I think carefully on these themes, I verbalize that I am grateful for whatever details come to mind. That's my gratitude adjustment. Generally, my attitude and feelings are completely reoriented by the time I'm done with the exercise. Often I don't even finish the whole thing. It could take 30 seconds or it could take five minutes. Depends on how I'm feeling. Of course, I return to this practice as needed no matter where I am. I can tell you it's really hard to be angry or bitter while simultaneously expressing thanks.

Again, I don't think there is magic in any particular recipe or ritual for practicing gratitude. The benefits flow first from being aware that you're not as grateful as you should be and second from being intentional about giving thanks. I'm tempted to say that none of this will work if your heart isn't in it. But the strange thing is that when we do something because it's good and right, our emotions and heart will soon follow. That was a diplomatic way of suggesting you should do this whether you feel like it or not.

GRATITUDE IS GROUND ZERO

When it comes to finding satisfaction, until we figure out our relationship with gratitude, we haven't figured out much at all. The journey to satisfaction starts when we embrace the challenge to grow our level of gratitude. I will promise you this: When you get gratitude right, you're going to get a lot of other things thrown in with it.

"It's really **hard to be angry**
or **bitter while** simultaneously
expressing thanks."

"Gratitude is not only the greatest of virtues, but
the parent of all others."

–Cicero

Practicing gratitude will change your life. It will change
the way you respond to circumstances because it will
change the very lens by which you see the world.

Dr. Brené Brown is a research professor at the
University of Houston Graduate College of Social Work.
She has spent 13 years studying vulnerability, courage,
worthiness, and shame. She offered the following on
gratitude:

"I think the relationship between joy and gratitude
was one of the most important things I found in the research. I wasn't expecting it, but I found in 12 years of
research (11,000 pieces of data), I did not interview, in
all that time, a person who would describe themselves
as joyful or describe their lives as joyous who did not
actively practice gratitude. For me this was very coun-
terintuitive; I went into the research thinking that the
relationship between joy and gratitude was 'if you are
joyful then you should be grateful,' but it wasn't that
way at all, it was really that 'practicing gratitude invites
joy into our lives."

When I listen to or meet high achievers that live in
ways I admire and would be willing to emulate, they all
have a relationship with gratitude. Conversely, when I
see high achievers crash and burn, and I listen to their
death-spiral stories, the topic of gratitude never comes up

and is generally missing from their lives entirely. Perhaps you've noticed that as well.

I recall looking around my church on a typical Sunday morning several years ago as people joined together in songs of worship. On stage, playing percussions, was a woman who had experienced an unbelievably deep loss — her daughter disappeared a decade prior, and years later her remains were discovered. It was determined that her daughter had been murdered. Near me, another couple, retired pastors, worshipped with arms lifted heavenward. Their son, who suffered from a mental illness, was shot and killed by police after he turned his gun on an officer following an episode at their own home. All around me I could see people who had walked through real pain and were practicing gratitude in their own way. The reality of what I was seeing that day made my problems seem smaller.

Since we have a church theme going here...I recall something Pastor Rick Warren has said more than once. "I used to think that life was hills and valleys — you go through a dark time, then you go to the mountaintop, back and forth. I don't believe that anymore. Rather than life being hills and valleys, I believe that it's kind of like two rails on a railroad track, and at all times you have something good and something bad in your life. No matter how good things are in your life, there is always something bad that needs to be worked on. And no matter how bad things are in your life, there is always something good you can thank God for."

Gratitude is a matter of focus, not a matter of circumstances.

THE GATEWAY TO GRACE

You've no doubt heard the term "mutually beneficial." A mutually beneficial exchange is where both parties get something in the deal. It's a common practice that makes economies and families work.

When we begin to practice gratitude by giving thanks, we naturally move into a mental posture that can make some uncomfortable. Once we take the time to do an inventory of blessings we've *received*, we discover that we're on the receiving end of a one-sided beneficial exchange. Upon reflection, we must determine that we have natural gifts, resources, and blessings that we didn't earn.

This realization presents challenges and opportunities. Without getting either too cosmic or too spiritual, the idea of expressing thanks begs the question of *to whom*?

I was having dinner with a friend and mentor when our conversation turned to gratitude. He's a brilliant and wealthy entrepreneur, and he let me know that he practices gratitude every day by giving thanks. I asked him, *"To whom?"* Without hesitation he shot back, "Who cares?!?" I chuckle at his candor and his reluctance to ascribe to a particular faith. Like my pal, whether you choose to name the source of your blessings or choose to express thanks to a nameless force, that's up to you.

Recognizing there is a source to be acknowledged and thanked is paramount to your growth for two reasons: First, because it's important for ambitious people to discover they aren't the deity. Shocking, I know. Many of us are immersed in the practice of "if it is to be, it's up to me." We convince ourselves that we have to work nonstop or at least longer and harder than the next guy to get what we need in this life. How we actually behave, regardless of what we say, is as if we believe all the good things we currently enjoy were a result of our own hard work and intelligence. Of our own *creation*. Ambitious leaders need to be set free from the trap of acting like we are holding the world together. We can learn this through gratitude, or we can learn it from trials and tragedy that will humble us to the point we understand our true position in the universe. At least we have a choice!

The second reason why it's important to acknowledge and thank a source is that we will begin to discover abundance thinking. In his classic book, *The 7 Habits of Highly Effective People*, Steven R. Covey coined the idea of *abundance mentality* or *abundance mindset*, a concept in which a person believes there are enough resources and successes to share with others. He contrasts it with the *scarcity mindset* (i.e., destructive and unnecessary competition), which is founded on the idea that if someone else wins or is successful in a situation, that means you lose; not considering the possibility of all parties winning (in some way or another) in a given situation. Individuals with an abundance mentality reject the notion of zero-sum games and are able to celebrate the success of others rather than feel threatened by it.[vii] Ambitious people are often afraid that somehow they won't have their needs met. Covey suggests that abundance and scarcity are opposite mindsets, and we get to choose which one to embrace.

When we practice gratitude, we become more receptive to new and positive changes. We can choose to let go of being fearful, defensive, hardened, or demanding through recognizing what we've already received and believing there is even more on the way.

"Gratitude is happiness doubled by wonder."
—G. K. Chesterton

AN ENTITLEMENT ANTIDOTE

Entitled people think they deserve special treatment. Gifted and driven people, especially those with financial resources, can start to believe their own publicity and get a taste for the finer things. Whether we become travel snobs (No, your bag goes above *your* seat in the back of the plane!) or we simply refuse to wait in lines...these attitudes come easy. We begin to feel like the rules apply to others, but perhaps not to us.

Raising affluent kids in an environment where entitlement is not consciously combated with gratitude is setting them up for a rude settlement with reality. They may have money, but their relationships and influence will suffer as entitlement erodes their character. Developing a heart for gratitude now sets our kids up to manage their blessings later. Think of it like an affluenza vaccination.

However, "The old adage that virtues are caught, not taught, applies here," says University of California, Davis psychology professor Robert Emmons. Parents need to model this behavior to build their children's gratitude muscle. "It's not what parents want to hear, but you cannot give your kids something that you yourselves do not have," Dr. Emmons says.

A 2010 study examined 1,035 high school students out-side New York City. The study, published in the *Journal of Happiness Studies*, found that those who showed high levels of gratitude, for instance, thankfulness for the beauty of nature and strong appreciation of other people, reported having stronger GPAs, less depression and envy, and a more positive outlook than less grateful teens.

Further, teens who strongly connected buying and owning things with success and happiness reported having lower GPAs, more depression, and a more negative outlook. "Materialism had just the opposite effect as gratitude—almost like a mirror," says study co-author Jeffrey Froh, associate professor of psychology at Hofstra University. Almost like a mirror...or two sides of the same coin.[viii]

GRATITUDE IS ENOUGHNESS

In 2014, I took a trip to Barcelona for the world's preeminent wireless industry trade show. It was my first European adventure, and I loved it. One of my memories from that trip came during a lonely, late-night walk. Normally, I'd hang out with industry colleagues, but on this night I went for a walk in the neighborhood near our hotel.

I was alone in a trendy foreign city where I was essentially anonymous. There were temptations all around. I felt the strong pull to check the local nightlife scene to see what kind of excitement might be on the other side of those doors. I kept walking. Thankfully, the closer I got to my hotel, the more pleased I was with my decision. And, as I walked, I had this thought: *Lust is the voice of ingratitude*. Much more than inappropriate sexual desire, lust speaks on behalf of ingratitude because it whispers, and, at times, shouts that *what I am, what I have, and what I feel* are not enough.

These lies will lead us to great heartache if we listen.

"I am not enough" leads to insecurity and holds us back from our potential.

"I don't have enough" drives us toward greed and envy.

"What I feel isn't enough" leads us toward moral compromises of every kind.

Gratitude is enoughness and flips the table on lust by focusing on all that we *do* have.

GRATITUDE LEADS TO CONTENTMENT

We don't become grateful when we are satisfied. We become satisfied when we are grateful.

Studies show that grateful people are happier and more satisfied with their lives and social relationships. They are more forgiving and supportive than those who are ungrateful. They are less depressed, stressed, envious, and anxious. In fact, high levels of gratitude explain more about psychological well-being than 30 of the most commonly studied personality traits, according to two recent studies published in the journal, *Personality and Individual Differences*.[ix] In the research leading up to these journal findings, 389 participants were asked to complete a series of questions dealing with three areas: how grateful they were, their personality type, and their satisfaction with life. Researchers concluded "that gratitude has a unique relationship with satisfaction with life."[x] Being grateful

"We **don't become grateful**
when we are **satisfied**. We **become**
satisfied **when** we are **grateful**."

affected participants' satisfaction with life even more than their personality type. Interestingly, gratitude and satisfaction are so closely related that some effort went into determining if they were basically the same idea. Research says...no, they're not the same. In my experience, one drives the other; gratitude drives satisfaction.

There are entire fields of research cropping up to focus on what is called positive psychology, which is the scientific study of the strengths and virtues that enable individuals and communities to thrive. The field is founded on the belief that people want to lead meaningful and fulfilling lives, to cultivate what is best within themselves, and to enhance their experiences of love, work, and play.[xi] Whether it's practicing "mindfulness" or the benefits of learning to "savor" the things that bring pleasure to your life. I find it a fascinating area of study because the practical applications for ambitious people are easy, and the benefits are immediate.

Gratitude works like a muscle. Take time to recognize good fortune, and feelings of appreciation can increase. Even more, those who are less grateful gain the most from a concerted effort. "Gratitude treatments are most effective in those least grateful," says Eastern Washington University psychology professor, Philip Watkins.[xii]

Did you catch that? Dr. Watkins says "gratitude treatments" are most effective in those least grateful. That's good news for highly ambitious people who naturally focus on their desires at the expense of gratitude. When we are burdened and emotionally spent from our striving, gratitude can feel like a desert rain, quenching our thirst and bringing back the colors of life.

Contentment and satisfaction live on the other side of gratitude.

"**Contentment** and **satisfaction live**
on the **other side of gratitude.**"

CHAPTER 7
Motivation and Purpose

Gratitude changes everything. It resets reality. We find the necessary emotional stability, if only for a moment's time, to ask ourselves deeper questions. Questions about what's bothering us and what's driving us. Big questions about purpose and calling and the kind of leaders we want to be.

Picture a horse and carriage galloping through the English countryside. Take a deep breath…visualize this scene. Now, ask yourself whether you identify most with the horse, the carriage, or the driver.

—The horse goes where commanded.
—The carriage is along for the ride.
—The driver calls the shots.

Are you driving, or just driven? Do you know what's driving you? Do you spend time asking why you do the things you do and feel the things you feel? I shared my story about growing up in a commune to provide some context, but also because, over time, I realized it was while in the commune that I developed a chip on my shoulder and belief that I had to prove myself. My dysfunction was driving me. Along the way, I also developed somewhat of an adrenaline addiction. I always wanted to be doing something, taking on so much that I was almost always too anxious to rest.

Growing up we had just one TV station, so some of our best entertainment was VHS tapes of the Three Stooges... Curly, Larry, and Moe. I've shown my kids this slapstick comedy of yesteryear. It's far from politically correct, to the point they shoot me a look to ask, "Is this okay?" In one skit, all three stooges are visiting a hospital when Curly breaks forth in his finest, and loudest, opera voice.

Curly: (sings opera) eeyaaaa, gibbity foootttt, la ciii, yaaaa nyuk, nyuk, nyuk.

Moe: (pokes Curly in the eyes)

Curly: Whoa! Oh! Moe! Moe! I can't see! I can't see!

Moe: Whatsa matta?

Curly: (smiling) I got my eyes closed.

Moe: (pokes Curly again)[xiii]

Often, ambitious people aren't able to see what's driving us because we're not willing to examine our true feelings and motivations. Like Curly, we're claiming blindness while all along we've got our eyes tightly closed. We don't take enough time to be introspective, and the idea of talking about these things openly with another human scares us to death. We get lots of accolades for our high performance, but do we know what's keeping us up at night? Have we figured out why we wake up with a rush of anxiety?

Behind the scenes, ambitious people often struggle with powerful and unhealthy emotions. It's been said that stress is what achievers call fear. I've observed that our fear often masquerades as diligence. We're afraid, so we work harder while trying to convince ourselves and others what we're doing is necessary. Peter Senge, author of the leadership classic, *The Fifth Discipline*, observed that for some, "Even when they achieve their goals, they immediately begin worrying about losing what they have gained."

As we've discussed, sometimes our ambition is really *envy*. Often our anger is really *feeling sorry for ourselves*. Or maybe we're known for always seeking a better mate, belief system, or opportunity while we're really just *scared to commit* in case it doesn't work. Becoming our best selves requires asking hard questions that get beyond our surface emotions or our carefully maintained image we want people to see. A commitment to relentlessly pursue the truth about what's driving us allows us to challenge the habits and false beliefs that hold us back.

> Well, maybe if I could see
> What's pushin' and pullin', poundin' on me
> Maybe I could take a step-by-step self evaluation
> I could find the ultimate underlying no-denying motivation
>
> —Wes King

What's driving you?

"I've observed that our **fear often masquerades as diligence.**"

THE CURVATURE OF THE EARTH

My business associate, Tarka L'Herpiniere, is a unique combination of world-class adventurer and software guru. Tarka is one of the most driven people I've ever met. He's climbed Everest, run ultra-marathons, and walked the entire Great Wall of China. In 2014, Tarka and his British travel mate, Ben Saunders, spent 105 days walking across Antarctica completing the Scott Expedition, an iconic 1,795-mile route from the coast of Antarctica to the South Pole and back, making it the longest polar man-haul in history.

I recall having a fascinating conversation with Tarka in the heart of Silicon Valley just days after he returned from pushing the outer limits of his physical and mental endurance. Over edamame and tiger rolls, Tarka described the extreme mental challenge of trekking into the sterile and seemingly endless white for close to four months. They plowed forward day after day into the featureless desert, devoid of all life, living in temperatures as low as -58F with only the horizon to aim for. Can you believe Tarka was coding from the tundra?

Since Tarka is one of those rare individuals who's stood on top of most of the world's tallest mountains and at the Poles, he's seen some views most of us haven't. Scientifically speaking, given enough altitude, you can see the curvature of the earth. Practically, it can be demonstrated by looking out of the window of a 747. However, according to Tarka, seeing the earth curving away from you from an icy windswept ledge at 29,000 feet somehow looks different.

Whether objects that seem to disappear over the horizon is an illusion related to our ability to see that far or a result of the actual curvature (=8 inches per mile squared), this image of the curvature of the earth is how I imagine ambitious people setting our goals. Figuratively, we look toward the horizon and plant a flag at the edge of our vision—a stretch goal tied to some worthy cause, an asset we want to possess, or an achievement intended to bring us satisfaction. However, on our way to this flag, things seem to change. Just at the point our flag (original goal) comes into focus, we catch glimpses of another flag (new goal), just barely visible on the edge of a new horizon. On our journey, the earth has curved under our feet and now we see something more. Almost instantly, the emotional energy and purpose tied to our original goal begins to dissipate while our interest and affections shift towards the newly-visible flag. The new goal...out there, on the new horizon.

In his excellent book, *Rescuing Ambition*, author Dave Harvey addresses this problem (by quoting C. H. Spurgeon):

> Ambition is a tricky thing, isn't it? We think greatness is attainable, so we work hard to attain it. But, like Alexander (the Great), as soon as we think we've reached it, we discover something that is greater, beyond our reach. There is always a nicer lawn in the neighborhood, a smarter kid in the class, a better golfer on the course...

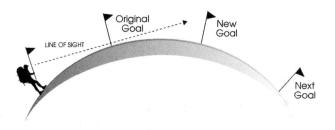

Almost instantly, the **emotional energy and purpose tied to our original goal** begins to **dissipate** while our **interest and affections shift** toward the **newly-visible flag**. The **new goal...out there**, on the **new horizon**.

See Alexander's tears! He weeps! Yes, he weeps for another world to conquer! Ambition is insatiable! The gain of the whole world is not enough. Surely to become a universal monarch is to make one's self universally miserable.

THE POWER OF A NEW AFFECTION

Why is ambition insatiable? Because there is an endless parade of objects to set our affections upon. And when we fall in love with something, everything else suddenly fades into the backdrop. Dr. Thomas Chalmers, a professor of moral philosophy at St. Andrews University in the early 1800s, introduced this idea in an oration entitled, "The Expulsive Power of a New Affection." It's written in historical language, so you may want to read it twice.

> ...the boy ceases, at length, to be the slave of his appetite; but it is because a manlier taste has now brought it into subordination, and that the youth ceases to idolize pleasure; but it is because the idol of wealth has become the stronger and gotten the ascendency, and that even the love of money ceases to have the mastery over the heart of many a thriving citizen; but it is because, drawn into the whirl of city politics, another affection has been wrought into his moral system, and he is now lorded over by the love of power. **There is not one of these transformations in which the heart is left without an object.** Its desire for one particular object may be conquered; but as to its desire for having some one object or other, this is unconquerable.

As Dave Harvey explains, "This ability to perceive, prize, and pursue is part of our essential humanness, and it's the essence of ambitions. Ambitions rise to what we prize."[xiv]

So, let's bring this point home. If the object of our new affection will push everything aside, and if our ambitions will rise to what we prize, the message for ambitious leaders is this: We should be very intentional in what we aim for.

LIVING ON PURPOSE

The Purpose Driven Life is the most successful book ever written on finding your purpose. Author Rick Warren, who I mentioned earlier, has said, "I think that the difference between what I call the survival level of living, the success level of living, and the significance level of living is do you figure out 'what on earth am I here for?'"

I can't fully do justice to the notion of finding your unique purpose in these final chapters of a book about ambition and gratitude. It's a huge and important topic because I believe achievement disconnected from purpose will always be unfulfilling.

But, after we discover gratitude and take a deep look at what's been driving us, I can think of no better use of our energies than getting clear about our purpose in life. I can't define your purpose for you, and neither can anyone else. You have to do the hard work of thinking through what makes you tick and where your vocation intersects with your inspiration. You have to assess whether faith will play a role in your life or if you will rely solely on observed science. You have to assess your hard wiring, your gifts, and your "calling." There are no shortcuts, but there are many who have gone before you in this process of getting clear about their own purpose and reorganizing their priorities and activities accordingly. I recommend that you find a mentor to help you answer the question of purpose to your own satisfaction.

Everything can and should be measured against our purpose. We have to take the time to contemplate our gifting, our connections, our education, our resources, and our passions in order to figure out our purpose. Our goals and our whys behind our goals need to tie back to that purpose. If they don't, then practice the art of quitting—quit the things that have no connection to your purpose. Life will get simpler and you'll find more margin to focus on what truly matters to you. Life is too short to chase other people's goals and purposes. Chase your own.

During those years following the sale of the first business, I really didn't like who I'd become. Being young with free time and a fair amount of cash had afforded me the opportunity to sample life in the fast lane. I'd constructed a great outward image, but, internally, I wasn't comfortable in my own skin. I was struck with a powerful question that went right to the heart of what was ailing me. The question was this: "Did I want to be a man of integrity or just be known as a man of integrity?" The thought came into my mind with such clarity that it was impossible to avoid. During that same time period, I recall being on horseback above the meandering Madison River in Montana when I came to an important conclusion about what I valued most in life. Despite all of the success, experiences, and material goods that had flowed through my hands, the thing I wanted most in life was a clean conscience. And, at that particular moment, I didn't have one. It took a while to clean up my messes, but with plenty of help from others, I got there.

Wrestling with gratitude had brought me clarity about where I really was and the changes I needed to make. I developed a strong desire to actually *live* according to my values, and I felt a renewed sense of purpose and humility. Note, I'm not claiming to be humble. But, over the years, thankfully, I've been humbled often enough to finally appreciate the opportunities I have to be a person of influence. I want to make the most of those opportunities, and I believe you do, too.

"Did I want to be a **man of integrity or** just be **known as** a **man of integrity?**"

CHAPTER 8
Reaching for Your Potential

Leading with gratitude is our response to the reality that we have been entrusted with gifts to utilize and opportunities to pursue. A gratitude adjustment and getting clear on what's been driving us brings renewed vigor, while at the same time, a sense of contentment and satisfaction. I am not referring to the kind of contentment that comes as if we have settled for the status quo or achieved all of our goals, but, instead, an internal confirmation that we're doing what we're supposed to be doing, and doing it for the right reasons.

By the time this race is over, I'd like to have run it well enough that, without stretching the truth, this single (run-on!) sentence will be chiseled on my tombstone: "He reached for his potential, he impacted his world, and he left a legacy."

REACH FOR YOUR POTENTIAL

IMPACT YOUR WORLD

LEAVE A LEGACY

We're going to tackle these three ideas individually in the remaining pages of this book. We will start with how we lead ourselves, shift toward how we impact others, and discuss how we leave a legacy that carries on when we've moved on.

"Someday people will summarize your life in a single sentence. My advice: pick it now!"—John Maxwell

Did you notice this chapter is titled, "Reaching *for* Your Potential" and not, "Reach Your Potential"? Including that one word changes the meaning dramatically. This reflects one of my own core values—progress. If, from a new position of gratitude, we're going take seriously the challenge to become effective leaders, we have to start with a commitment to personal growth. It's difficult to lead others to places we haven't been or to teach lessons we haven't internalized and applied in our own life. Not only does it feel hypocritical to do so, but we run out of juice if we aren't continually learning and growing as leaders.

Many ambitious leaders live with tremendous pressure to meet their *own* expectations. They wake with it in the morning and sleep with it at night. There are few burdens heavier than the burden of potential and few disappointments as profound as feeling like we didn't live up to our potential.

Truth be told, we will reach *for* our potential, but we will never really hit it. When I imagine the most glorious version of my future and call that *my potential*, the gap between my reality (or worst moments) is so wide that it's utterly demoralizing. By adding the word *for* to the mix, I'm consciously reminding myself that I'm on a journey. I give myself the grace to screw up as long as I get back up. I reject the idea that I need to be perfect, but I cling hard to the idea that I need to be aiming at excellence and *making progress*.

Furthermore, our capacity as leaders and humans is often much greater than we imagine. A finite, fixed potential would be horrible. Who really wants to hear they've already lived up to their potential? That's a bit like being told nobody expected much from you anyhow. Ambitious people don't like being put in boxes of any kind. Telling us we can't do something is like putting red meat in front of a hungry lion.

Our task isn't to measure the limits of our potential, but to push ourselves to grow as leaders. After we make a realistic assessment of our capabilities and the opportunities in front of us, we must take courageous steps in that direction. And, on the journey, we need to celebrate the small victories as a tangible way to remind ourselves that, even though we're not where we want to be, we are making progress.

LIVING IN TENSION

Peter Senge says, "Most of us hold one of two contradictory beliefs that limit our ability to create what we want. The more common belief is our powerlessness—our inability to bring into being all the things we really care about. The other belief centers on unworthiness—that we do not deserve to have what we truly desire."

Senge works closely with Robert Fritz, an accomplished composer, filmmaker, and writer, who is also an organizational consultant for some of the largest companies in the world. Together, they teach a metaphor to describe how these "contradictory underlying beliefs" work as a system, counter to achieving our goals. Imagine, as you move toward your goal, there is a rubber band, symbolizing creative tension, pulling you in the desired direction. But imagine also a second rubber band, anchored to the belief of powerlessness or unworthiness. Just as the first rubber band tries to pull you toward your goal, the second rubber band pulls you back toward the underlying belief that you can't (or don't deserve) to have your goal.[xv]

PERSONAL MASTERY

Source: Fifth Discipline

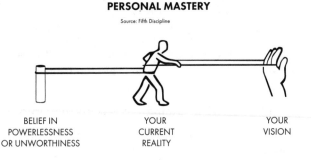

BELIEF IN	YOUR	YOUR
POWERLESSNESS	CURRENT	VISION
OR UNWORTHINESS	REALITY	

Ambitious leaders often live with this tension. We set grand goals, but we live in view of the familiar things that keep pulling us back. When we set ambitious goals, we will be racked with emotions that come upon us like floods. That's not a sign of weakness, it's a sign of humanity. How we respond to these emotions makes all the difference in the world. One of the reasons that a gratitude practice is so helpful in combating the negative emotions that leaders face is that gratitude reorients us to truth, to correct thinking about why we are neither powerless nor unworthy.

"When we **set ambitious goals**,
we will be **racked with emotions**
that **come upon us like floods**. That's
not a sign of weakness, it's a **sign
of humanity**."

COMMIT TO PERSONAL GROWTH

> "Success is peace of mind, which is a direct result of self-satisfaction in knowing you made the effort to become the best you are capable of becoming."
> —John Wooden

Aleksandr Solzhenitsyn was sentenced to a Soviet Gulag (labor camp) for eight years after being accused of producing anti-Soviet propaganda in private letters that were critical of Stalin's war. He entered prison an atheist and emerged a man of faith. Looking back, he said,

> "I bless you, prison—I bless you for being in my life— for lying therein on the rotting prison straw, I learned the object of life is not prospering as I had grown up believing, but the maturing of the soul."

Reaching for our potential is really a "maturing of the soul." It's deep and it's lasting, bringing a sense of purpose to our lives.

I want to be surrounded by people who are reaching for their potential and taking action toward the maturing of their souls.

DISCOVER YOUR STRENGTHS

A key component of understanding your potential as a leader is making the time to assess your personality and leadership style. For people who have never done this, it can seem a little touchy-feely on one hand and clinical on the other. Just go with it. The process of self-discovery is key to personal growth and maximum impact as a leader.

In our efforts to form a cohesive leadership team in my last company, we used the assessment from Stand-Out as a tool for discovering and playing to our individual leadership strengths. My StandOut revealed that I am strongest as a Connector and Creator. That explains why, by nature, I am energized at trade events and tend to generate a lot of ideas to kick around rather than spend time perfecting current operations. As a leader, I've used StandOut to remind me of the leadership strengths and biases of my team. These insights allow me to tailor initiatives toward the giftedness of others, make sure to avoid areas where they struggle, and remind myself of how to work best with them. One of my partners always struck me as a complete control freak. When I realized his greatest strength was as a Protector, it helped me appreciate how his focus on policy and process really served the team in areas that we all needed. Applying gratitude to the process caused me to slow down and appreciate the diverse strengths of others, especially when people with styles different than mine were driving me crazy!

StandOut worked for us, but a quick search will yield a variety of tried-and-true assessment tools including, perhaps the most common, the Myers-Briggs Type Indicator. The value comes in learning about yourself and how to work collaboratively with people who have different styles, gifts, and preferences.

If you haven't yet spent much time working on defining your strengths, consider taking these steps:

1. Take a strengths or personality assessment. Then, find a person invested in your success and discuss what your assessment indicates about your unique personality and strengths. Many people initially resist these exercises because they are afraid of being put in a box or labeled a certain way. From my experience, the valuable discussions following a strengths assessment far outweigh the risk of having the information used to manipulate you.

2. Don't agonize over your weaknesses. You're better off finding ways to grow your strengths than you are patching up your weaknesses. Be real about your gaps, take corrective action if necessary, and partner with people who have the strengths you're in need of.

My daughter and I enjoyed hearing a great speech from John Maxwell at a leadership conference in Australia. He sought to liberate us from obsessing over the areas where we suck. He argues that on a scale of one to 10, there are areas where each of us falls below a five. He proposes that rather than try to improve in an area where we have no apparent talent or passion, we instead invest in areas where we have natural strength and passion to see if we can't move the needle up to an eight or even a nine. Summary paraphrase: "Improving yourself to a six in an area

"Don't agonize over your **weaknesses."**

may be admirable, but people will *stand in line for a nine.*"
Don't obsess over or try to patch your weaknesses. Focus
on your strengths to make the biggest gains.

3.   Look for roles that fit your strengths and allow
      them to shine. Regardless of the title, you'll be
      happiest when you connect with your strengths
      and commit to grow them.

Things get really sweet when we're good at something
but also happen to enjoy it. A whole team of people living
at the intersection of their competence and passion would
be unstoppable.

FIND A MENTOR

Since we don't work out our growth alone, you need to
decide who you trust to impart counsel and perspective
into your life. Find mentors, but don't bother to call them
that. Trying to find mentoring can turn into an awkward
dance of misaligned expectations. Rather, locate subject
matter experts you trust, and find a way to spend time
with them or learn from them indirectly.

Look for people you admire, who have been where you
want to go, and build real relationships over the long haul.

Don't be needy. Successful people don't open up if they
feel they will be used or get entangled before they choose
to.

When I started with my most recent company, I retained a leadership coach to help mentor me. I'd begun
meeting with Rick Graham informally before I took the

job leading a small company that I'd invested in. He had a background as a corporate facilitator with Hewlett Packard and moved to Southern Oregon to raise a family. In one of our earliest meetings, I remember Rick telling me that I had "what it takes" to lead the company. I *really* needed to hear that word of encouragement at the time. I'd just come off getting obliterated with a handful of failed ventures and my confidence was completely rattled. I was wrestling with those limiting beliefs, and the wounds of failure were still fresh.

Rick and I committed to meet weekly as schedules permitted, and I found the time invaluable. I had a sounding board to bounce ideas off of, to ask questions of, to hold myself accountable to. Plus, Rick eats good books for breakfast, so I had a steady diet of classic and new ideas to consider. I remember early on, he asked me what I wanted out of the coaching relationship. I recall having two objectives: to lead with authenticity, and to have my team say that, as a leader, I had focused on the right things.

It's a good thing I found a mentor because I really needed one. Actually, I ended up with several because the company we started experienced explosive growth, and we needed all the brainpower and experience we could get our hands on. We had a tiger by the tail. Over the next eight years following that meeting with Rick, we grew our little company from an idea to a national leader with revenue approaching $60,000,000 and top talent scattered across the nation. I could talk for weeks about the tactical and strategic challenges we navigated. It felt to me like a great responsibility and, to help me reach for my potential, I treasured having someone to help me define what I believed about leadership and how to bring that to life.

FACE DOWN THE RESISTANCE

Be forewarned, when you set goals in big, scary, or creative areas, you will immediately face resistance. Breaking through the atmosphere toward orbit is violent, turbulent, and hot. So it is with your growth journey. Often when we commit to reaching toward our potential, we will experience serious opposition before we break through.

When we commit to growth in any area of our life that matters to our soul, we will encounter resistance in a variety of insidious forms:

Our own voice…telling us to
stay in our own sandbox!

Others' voices…pointing out all
the barriers to success.

Our own habits…keeping us
sidelined and unproductive.

Others' habits…getting in our way.

"Rule of thumb: The more important a call or action is to our soul's evolution, the more resistance we will feel toward pursuing it." —Steven Pressfield, *The War of Art*

We can withstand almost any adversity as long as we're pursuing something that truly matters to us and we're seeing progress. Great satisfaction comes from knowing we are among those with the courage to reach for our potential.

"**Great satisfaction** comes
from **knowing** we are among those
with the **courage** to **reach for
our potential**."

CHAPTER 9
Impact Your World

The last chapter should have gone down easy because it's about us. We like us. Now it's time to turn the corner and shift our attention to others.

Ambition has a default setting of self. What do I need? What do I want? What do I fear? What can I accomplish? Leadership, by definition, implies a focus on others. Regularly expressing gratitude for the "cast of characters" who surround us will adjust our focus beyond our own needs and onto the opportunity we have to lead others.

Dr. Froh, who I mentioned earlier, says, "Being other focused is a prerequisite to being grateful. It allows you to focus on the relationships and goodness in your life because of other people. A major source of gratitude is our loved ones. If you ask people what they're thankful for, nine out of 10 times the first several things they're going to say are people."[xvi]

You've noticed this chapter is titled, "Impact Your World." The emphasis here is on *your world* and not *the world at large*. Often we get wrapped up in trying to make a name for ourselves or tackle grand, even global, issues. All the while, we're missing the opportunities to make a huge impact on those standing right by our side—people who we actually know. Thinking about others brings us to gratitude, and gratitude compels us to lead others well.

We like the glamour and mystery of great goals, but we may be striving for these visions with no real way of determining our impact. Leadership that makes the most lasting impact takes place face to face with the people near you. If we're overlooking investing in relationships with the people in our life (especially our own family) because we are focused on chasing a "greater cause," we've got it backwards. Unless we find ourselves in another world war, there is no greater cause than the people nearest you who look to you as a leader.

Leading with gratitude requires that we break out of the mental model that places us on the white horse, saving the day. We move past the idea that we're the smartest person in the room, and we take on the responsibility of building up the people around us. This is a sign that we are transitioning from the role of individual contributor to the role of an intentional leader.

BE THE MENTOR YOU WISH YOU HAD

In Chapter 8, we talked about finding a mentor. I believe this is critical to our success as grateful leaders. However, of equal importance is becoming a mentor to those who look up to you. Many of us can get so focused on growing our own skills to reach for our own potential that we rush past people who would benefit from what we've already learned. In the same way, *we* don't want to learn every lesson the hard way, we have an obligation to share our insights with the receptive high-potential people that are drawn into our life.

I mentioned my ill-fated venture into franchising. Personally, I think franchises are a horrible model for entrepreneurs unless you're the franchisor! Over the years,

"**Leading with gratitude** requires that we **break out of the mental model** that places us on the **white horse**, saving the day."

I've had several friends share their ideas about buying a franchise, and I've successfully discouraged them from going down that road. I grab them by the ears and force them to look me in the eyes while I recount my own horror stories. (Well, not exactly, but close enough.) No sense in all of us learning the hard way.

It's been said that the Dead Sea is dead because it has no outlet. All it does it take in water, never releasing it. That's a good leadership analogy for mentoring. There is health in the balance that comes from the giving and taking of mentoring.

In this phase of my life, I keep an office in a co-working space full of young(ish) entrepreneurs. We learn from each other, bringing to bear our skills and experiences in a vibrant type-A community. It's a joy to be able to share some of my hard-fought lessons with young leaders before they break their toes on the same rocks I've already kicked. I learn a lot from them, too.

Additionally, I've been able to assist a variety of small, non-profit organizations with a combination of modest charitable gifts paired with practical operational insights gleaned from healthy business organizations. Occasionally, I've met resistance for trying to push a non-profit too hard. "You're trying to run this non-profit like a corporation," one board member decried. After a few days pondering his comment, I came to a conclusion: No, in fact, I was simply trying to push this non-profit to become a healthy organization. He'd constructed a false dichotomy that business and non-profits don't operate under the same principles. I'd been doing a lot of work on organizational health using Patrick Lencioni's work, and I eventually concluded a leadership change would be necessary for this non-profit to become a healthy organization. Had I not been through my own battles in business, I would not have had the conviction to stay the course when things became extremely difficult.

Other non-profits I work with have great impact, but they don't tell their story as well as they do their work. It's fulfilling to be able to introduce them to top-talent resources from the business world who can help them highlight all they do. If we have our eyes open, we discover there are myriad mentoring opportunities all around us if we're willing to get our hands dirty.

When we are blessed financially we often ratchet up our tastes and lifestyles in ways that can disconnect us from those who need our help. In other words, we want *clean* hands. Our social interactions, cars, clothes, and interests become barriers that separate us from the "G-POP" (general population). A grateful leader understands that their gifts (financial and experience) aren't solely for their own enjoyment. We are stewards with an obligation to give back.

Being an effective mentor is more than an occasional coffee. We all long for that world-class sage willing to take the time to impart wisdom and share their life with us. **Be the mentor you wish you had.**

RECOGNIZE YOUR INFLUENCE

Often, we become what people tell us we are. Our mental images of ourselves are influenced by the things others say about us, whether positive or negative. Think back

"Be the mentor you
wish you had."

in your life...did someone call out a character trait in you that came to define you? Did someone point out something about your body that you still think about to this day? I suspect so. Whether we like it or not, words have power, and words spoken by those with influence in our life can have superpowers.

Since this is a fact, it is time we start to apply it in reverse by recognizing there are many who admire, trust, and follow us. Our actions and the words we use, or refuse to say, can have a major impact on those around us.

However, no matter how profound we think our words and principles may be, who we are always has a greater impact than what we say. John Wooden was fond of sharing this poem he picked up in the 1930s:

> No written word nor spoken plea
> Can teach your team what they should be
> Nor all the books on all the shelves
> It's what the leader is himself

Just a few months ago, my father, Mark Buechley, passed away at the age of 69, following an intense battle with pancreatic cancer. I had the privilege of writing and delivering the eulogy at his celebration of life. Here is a bit of what I shared that day:

He was an intentional mentor. If he liked you, he'd encourage you. If he really liked you, he'd call you out on something, not to make you feel bad, but to call you to your best self. He would not look the other way and pretend he didn't notice. He would take action to reach into people's lives. My dad and I had a chance to make one last trip to Costa Rica. Over 10 days, we reconnected with many of his business associates and projects across the country. They would come when he requested, with tears in their eyes, knowing it would likely be the last time they would see Don Marcos. On this trip, I was an observer of the kind of impact he had wherever he went.

My dad loved people and had a keen sense of the influence he could have in people's lives. Nearly every time he took an airplane trip, he made a new friend.

Remember, truth, to have a positive impact, must be delivered in love. Otherwise, it's judgement. We don't point out people's flaws for the purpose of condemning them to that reality. We point out those "areas of improvement" because we genuinely want them to improve. Growing up in a cult, I observed truth being used to manipulate, control, and condemn. When we speak our truth to someone, we seek to mentor or influence, our *motive* must be love. And, if it's not, we should keep our observations to ourselves.

THE POWER OF A TEAM

Many ambitious leaders operate in frustration for two reasons: they don't identify what they are naturally good at, and they don't build a team capable of taking them farther than their own limited strengths. Being really good at something can be a blessing and a curse. A blessing when whatever we're good at is truly valuable to our business, but a curse when we rely too heavily on that

"Remember, **truth**, to have a **positive impact**, must be delivered in love."

talent without adding other talents to the mix. No matter how talented we are in one area, nobody gets all the gifts. Grateful leaders know their own strengths while learning how to appreciate, attract, and work with people who have completely different strengths.

If we want to grow our ventures past Mom & Pop, Inc., we must learn how to build well-rounded teams. In my businesses, I've effectively recruited people who were overlooked in larger companies. I simply promised an environment where self-motivated people had the chance to accelerate their individual growth without artificial barriers. People wanted to work where the culture allowed them to thrive and make a real impact. I truly believe this promise because I truly believe **leaders seek their own level**. Leaders want to know their career potential is in their hands. Confident leaders don't have to brag or fret when others get ahead because, eventually, we all end up at the level our leadership deserves. It's a universal truth. And when it doesn't appear that this is the case… just be patient long enough to let the universal truth play out. Eventually, the over-promoted person moves on, and the overlooked person moves up. If you see a turtle on a fence post, it's fair to conclude it didn't get there on its own. It won't stay there long either.

My last venture, SOLiD Technologies, USA, was to make the transition from being an individual contributor to being a leader of leaders. After getting clear on what we believed, we were able to start going after the talent we needed to grow the business. In the early years, it was hard slogging. We had to cajole our major supplier and technology partner to be patient with us while we built the infrastructure and culture of the organization while building sales momentum in the market.

The team started to gel after a few years, and, before long, we were adding about $1 million in revenue for every new employee! First 3, then 7, 15, 35, 58...we were rolling, and with practically no (voluntary) employee turnover over seven years.

What mattered to me throughout was that we'd accomplished what we set out to do—as a team. The people we'd recruited on the promise of being able to grow their leadership had, in fact, been given huge opportunities to elevate their careers by taking on increasing roles of responsibility. At least 100 times, I ended conversations with team members by asking, "Is there anything I can do to help you?" It was important to me that they knew my job was to serve them. And, in turn, they knew their job was to serve our customers and those who looked to them for leadership.

FOCUS ON CULTURE

When we set out to build our team at this last company, we had the benefit of starting from scratch. I discovered it's much easier to build a culture from scratch than it is to change a culture that pre-existed. Start-ups are a blank canvas, and we get to do our art, making a tapestry of these characters that get drawn to the cause. When we join a company or leadership team that is already in place, we have to mesh into the culture that exists and, perhaps, make incremental changes over time.

Coming into the opportunity to form a new venture, I knew that we would start with culture and go from there. We sat in a Starbucks in Las Vegas and talked about how we'd roll. This was our opportunity to take a shot at correcting what we'd seen other companies do wrong. Over time, we tweaked things a bit, but this is how we started to define those qualities important to our culture:

Creativity
There is always a way to solve a problem
or reset the circumstances.

Top Talent
We can become the best or hire the best.

Tell the Truth
Even when it hurts.

Innovation
See the need and develop a solution.

Channel Support
We rely on our channel (resellers) to survive.

Customer Service
Give the customers the benefit of the doubt
and win their loyalty.

Improvement
Maintain a culture of debrief to incorporate
lessons learned.

You might find "tell the truth" to be intriguing. In a sales-driven organization, you'd be surprised at how often that simple notion was tested. White lies are a way of life in much of the business world, and more than once I had key leaders challenge the gap between the words of our organization and our actions. This was a healthy process that, ultimately, built trust and credibility between the executive team and the management staff.

In Patrick Lencioni's bestseller, *The Advantage: Why Organizational Health Trumps Everything Else in Business*, he suggests, "The biggest reason that organizational health remains untapped is that it requires courage. Leaders must be willing to confront themselves, their peers, and the dysfunction within their organization with an uncommon level of honesty and persistence. They must be prepared to walk straight into uncomfortable situations and address issues that prevent them from realizing the potential that eludes them."[xvii] Stated differently, to impact our world, we have to get our hands dirty.

"To **impact our world**, we have to **get our hands dirty**."

CHAPTER 10
Leave a Legacy

You don't have to be dead to create a legacy. If you wait that long, you're too late.

I've thought a lot about the *idea* of legacy for years. I even formed a business and named it, "Legacy, LLC," just to try to keep a long-term perspective. There is definitely something in the DNA of an ambitious person that wants our influence to continue after we're gone. But I think we question our own motives about leaving a legacy, rightfully concerned that our underlying driver could be ego.

My friend, Jason Atkinson, and I were having a pleasant dinner in Portland when the conversation turned to the topic of legacy. Jason introduced me to Ozymandias. What? You haven't met him either? Ozymandias is a figure from a poem by Percy Bysshe Shelley.

When Jason introduced me to the poem, I looked it up on my mobile and asked him to narrate.

The summary: A traveler stumbles across "two vast trunkless" legs of stone in the middle of a barren desert… the torso of the statue lies nearby half buried in the sand, still sneering.

Never one to miss an opportunity for impact, suddenly Jason was on his feet in the middle of the restaurant *loudly* and appropriately delivering the punchline of the poem—the arrogant inscription on the crumbled statue:

My name is Ozymandias, King of Kings;

Look on my Works, ye Mighty, and despair!

The genteel patrons may have thought he was nuts, but do you think I'll ever forget the name of Ozymandias?

Truth is, a legacy oriented around our personal identity or glory lacks the power to inspire us because we know how false it is. I want to treat my legacy seriously, while not taking myself too seriously. Our physical presence on this hurling orb will soon end. Death is a reliable equalizer, even for someone as great as my new acquaintance, Ozymandias.

GROWING A LEGACY

"All that is not eternal is eternally useless."

—C. S. Lewis

I had several reasons for writing this book. A primary reason was for the benefit of my four children. I am committed to leaving them a *legacy of gratitude*. I don't even care if they get sick of the word, as long as they truly understand how it can be applied in their own lives to reorient them toward what is good and lasting. I'm also thinking about my grandkids before they are born.

Working on a legacy isn't something to be done *then,* when things slow down. We know that's a farce. Things never slow down for ambitious people because we don't really like it when they slow down. Legacy building begins now, by being intentional. We're here today and gone tomorrow, and if we won't take the steps to share the most important values in our life with the most important people in our life, nobody else is going to do it for us. It's not their job, it's ours.

It's a paradox that ambitious people spend so much energy chasing dreams to be achieved in this lifetime, with comparatively little action toward growing a *legacy which isn't bound by time*. We spend time on estate planning, but what about legacy planning? We invest in wills to pass along our assets, but how about something practical that passes along our values? Are we spending as much time avoiding entitlement in our kids as we do avoiding taxes? You get the point. Our opportunity to leave a legacy starts *now*, not when we're gone.

If we agree that ambitious people are those who want to make a difference, we should be able to agree that we'd like that difference to outlive us. You've likely been taught Covey's leadership principle of "start with the end in mind." Legacy is the end we should have in mind.

My friend, Aaron Larsen, is an expert on legacy. He teaches courses on *legacy gardening*, the process of cultivating meaningful relationships and growing rich legacies within yourself and your loved ones. He uses the analogy of a garden to highlight the necessary planning, planting, and care required to grow "patches" of one's life for the purpose of legacy. He writes, "How are these seeds planted? Through our words, thoughts, and actions! It's important to know that legacy gardening is an intentional and purposeful process. Just like in a real garden, you don't just toss seeds around willy-nilly everywhere, cross your fingers, and hope something good grows. You have to plan ahead and follow a clear and intentional process."

Within our sphere of influence and, particularly, within our family, we need to take practical action to invest in a legacy. Here are a few first step suggestions to consider:

- Develop hobbies and traditions to share with each of your children individually based on *their* interests. Consider the same for those you mentor as a way to spend time together in a less formal environment. An awful lot of life can be shared over a four-hour round of golf or a mountain bike ride. That's one reason retreats are so effective. They take us out of business constructs and often cross over into sharing life.

- Establish family traditions and imbue them with purpose, even if it feels corny. Perhaps once per week, ask members of the family to go around the table and share two things they are grateful for.

- Look up the phrase, "ethical will," and take a stab at drafting your own.

- Write out a "family mission statement" that moves past sentiment and toward the *why* and *how* your family wants to behave. Involve your kids and spouse in the process.

- Explore creating a digital history of the meaningful parts of your life using StoryCorps or similar.

Having walked alongside my dad during his final months, I regret not capturing even more of his story while he was at his best. When we're under stress or know our end is near, we will be too preoccupied to make these important legacy investments. Do it now.

A LEGACY OF VIRTUES

"It occurred to me that there were two sets of virtues, the résumé virtues and the eulogy virtues."

The quote above is from David Brooks' excellent *New York Times* op-ed, "The Moral Bucket List." He further expounds,

"If you live for external achievement, years pass and the deepest parts of you go unexplored and unstructured. You lack a moral vocabulary...you live with an unconscious boredom, separated from the deepest meaning of life and the highest moral joys. Gradually, a humiliating gap opens between your actual self and your desired self, between you and those incandescent souls you sometimes meet."

Our actions reveal what we believe, whether we like it or not. Too often, our actions reveal that we've oriented our lives around résumé building and financial success, rather than character building. No, they're not always mutually exclusive, but what we feed will grow, and what we starve will die. That's natural science as well as behavioral science.

The gist of Brooks' article is that without intentional focus we won't develop into the type of moral people we admire. Therefore, we also stand nearly no chance of defining or passing on those moral virtues to others. Brooks suggests we even "lack a moral vocabulary" to do so. Regardless of religious distinctions, most of us aspire to embody some sort of codified belief about what's right and wrong. We also desire to point our children, and those closest to us, in the "right" direction while leaving them plenty of flexibility to own their individual value system.

It's in these shared areas of morality, virtue, and struggling together that our greatest impact, our most lasting legacy, will be felt. Values are the heart of our legacy. Transferring values to children has always been a daunting challenge, but today it might be harder than ever. Being constantly connected to the world through technology means we are constantly tempted to disconnect from those closest to us. Too often, we spend our days scouring the digital pawn shop of our smartphone, while ignoring the treasures we already have, particularly at home.

I want to think about legacy like Melvin Maxwell does. Do you know who that is? How about Joshua Wooden? Ever heard of him? Let's try another…Theodore Roosevelt Sr.? By now, you've solved the riddle. Each of these men, along with their wives, raised some of the most respected leaders in the world.

In 2014, John Maxwell was named the No. 1 leadership and management expert in the world by *Inc. Magazine*. John's dad, Melvin, had an interesting way of making sure his kids reached their potential. Melvin theorized, "If I can fill your mind with the right thoughts, it'll be

"Too often, **we spend** our **days scouring** the **digital pawn shop** of our smartphone, while **ignoring** the treasures we **already have,** particularly at home."

amazing what you can accomplish in life. I put my money where my values are." What did he do? He curated good books full of leadership principles and actually paid his kids an allowance for reading them. John explains, "Our allowance was based on reading books. My parents would select the books, put them in our hands, and over the dinner table at night we would talk about what we were reading." Not only have I been the beneficiary of John Maxwell's leadership teaching through his many books, but my own leadership coach, Rick Graham, is a founding partner of the John Maxwell Team. Melvin, in his mid 90s, is still speaking and ministering in senior living facilities throughout the Southeast, and we're still reaping the benefit of his foresight and investment in developing the values of his children.

Many people know of John Wooden, considered one of the greatest basketball coaches ever. His UCLA Bruins won an incredible 10 national championships over a 12-year span. One of John Wooden's biggest influences in his life was his dad, Joshua Wooden. John Wooden explained how his dad gave him and his brothers simple rules to live by, all organized into what he called, "Two Sets of Threes." The first set was about honesty:

- Never lie.

- Never cheat.

- Never steal.

The second set dealt with adversity:

- Don't whine.

- Don't complain.

- Don't make excuses.

Then, when John Wooden graduated from elementary school, his dad gave him a $2 bill and a card. On one side of the card was this poem by Reverend Henry Van Dyke:

> Four things a man must learn to do
>
> If he would make his life more true:
>
> To think without confusion clearly,
>
> To love his fellow-man sincerely,
>
> To act from honest motives purely,
>
> To trust in God and Heaven securely.

On the other side of the card, Joshua Wooden wrote, "Seven Things to Do":

1. Be true to yourself.

2. Help others.

3. Make each day your masterpiece.

4. Drink deeply from good books, especially the Bible.

5. Make friendship a fine art.

6.   Build a shelter against a rainy day.

7.   Pray for guidance and give thanks for your blessings every day.[xviii]

Evidently, Joshua Wooden took his role as a moral mentor seriously. The resultant legacy of leadership still resonates in sports and beyond.

And, finally, we've already mentioned some the exploits of one of my favorite leaders, Teddy Roosevelt. Behind Teddy, there was Theodore Sr., who used his financial resources as a businessman to harness the natural ambition and intellect of young Teddy. He died at 46 years old, but, in that time, he laid the groundwork that helped fashion a man of tremendous strength and moral resolve. When sending young Teddy off to Harvard, Theodore Sr. provided this admonition: "Take care of your morals first, your health next, and finally your studies."

After his long and illustrious career, President Roosevelt wrote that it was good to build virtues that serve in the sphere of politics, but "these virtues are as dust in a windy street unless in back of them lie the strong and tender virtues of a family life based on the love of the one man for the one woman and on their joyous and fearless acceptance of their common obligation to the children that are theirs." Virtue. Love. Obligation.

Clearly, the investments of Melvin, Joshua, and Theodore Sr. have produced a legacy of virtue that continues to this day. Are we making the most of the opportunity we have to leave a legacy of virtues for those who follow us?

A LEGACY OF GRATITUDE

> Someday, somehow, someway,
> I'm gonna' be outa here.
>
> But when I go, will my work be done?
>
> Just how well will this race be run?

In delivering my father's eulogy, I was finally able to make sense of and put words to what I'd been seeing over the years. As the arc of his story unfolded, I was able to understand him as a young boy looking for love from his father. When he came to his own faith in the turbulent 60s, this emotional hole he carried began to fill. In time, he became a pillar of stability and encouragement to his family, but also dozens of people whom he came into contact with, mostly through his work, but also in his pursuit of fishing and horseback adventures in Montana and Costa Rica. He had a way of attracting and connecting with underdogs, and he made them believe that they could become something greater. Over the six months that we knew he had cancer, many people came—with a sense of urgency—to say goodbye and express appreciation for the impact he'd had on their life simply by offering a courageous word or act. He had a desire to give generously because he knew he'd been given so much.

Our ambition is a gift. Though I've brought into focus the attendant downsides of this personality trait, the world is made a better place by ambitious people who will not settle for the status quo. When we view ambition as a gift to be grateful for, we're more likely to appreciate it and harness it for lasting good. As we discussed, the leaders who make the biggest impact in the world are those who avoid getting burned by their own ambition, and who, instead, use it for the benefit of others.

Gratitude, perhaps unlike any other virtue, will not only position you for success, it will help you handle it and *actually enjoy it* when it shows up. Gratitude will free you from hoarding and stressing over the fear of loss because you'll know, at the deepest level, that what you have has been given to you, and you'll receive it as a gift to be cared for. When you discover the power of gratitude, you will experience changes in your personality, and even your motivations. You will *naturally* begin to think beyond yourself seeking to serve others in response to an acute awareness of all you have been given. From this new perspective you will enjoy greater levels of overall satisfaction and more frequent times of peace. You'll also be better positioned to reach for your potential, impact your world, and leave a legacy. As much as ever, this world truly needs ambitious people who will make the shift to *leading with gratitude.*

ENDNOTES

[i]William Smith, *Families and Communes: An Examination of Nontraditional Lifestyles* (SAGE Publications, 1999); p. 28.

[ii]Candice Millard, *The River of Doubt: Theodore Roosevelt's Darkest Journey* (Knopf Doubleday Publishing, 2009); intro.

[iii]Irving G. Schorsch III, "Too Much, Too Soon: How to Avoid Sudden Wealth Syndrome," *Huffington Post*, Sept. 06, 2012. Website.

[iv]*GetAbstract Summary*, (getAbstract, 2007), of William Bridges, *Transitions*, (Da Capo Press, 2004).

[v]Jason Franklin, "How Much is Enough?," classism.org, Dec. 06, 2011. Website.

[vi]Diana Kapp, "Raising Kids with an Attitude of Gratitude," *Wall Street Journal*, Dec. 23, 2013. Website.

[vii]*Wikipedia* overview, Stephen R. Covey, *The 7 Habits of Highly Effective People*, (Free Press, 1989). Website.

[viii]Diana Kapp, "Raising Kids with an Attitude of Gratitude," *Wall Street Journal*, Dec. 23, 2013. Website.

[ix]Mollie Ziegler Hemingway, "The Parent of All Virtues," *Christianity Today*, Nov. 28, 2010.

[x]Alex M. Wood, Stephen Joseph, John Maltby, "Gratitude uniquely predicts satisfaction with life: Incremental validity above the domains and facets of the five factor model," *Journal of Personality and Individual Differences*, Feb. 22, 2008.

[xi]"Positive Psychology," viacharacter.org. Website.

[xii]Diana Kapp, "Raising Kids with an Attitude of Gratitude," *Wall Street Journal*, Dec. 23, 2013. Website.

[xiii]*Three Stooges, Calling all Curs,* (Columbia Pictures, 1939).

[xiv]Dave Harvey, *Rescuing Ambition*, (Crossway, 2010).

[xv]Peter Senge, *The Fifth Discipline*, (Currency, 1990), p. 156.

[xvi]Interview with Dr. Jeffrey. J. Froh, Psy. D., Hofstra University, May 05, 2016.

[xvii]"Summary Article: The Last Competitive Advantage," tablegroup.com. Website.

[xviii]Jeffrey Pritchard, "Life Advice from John Wooden's Dad," allfinancialmatters.com. Website.

ABOUT THE AUTHOR

Ambition's author, Seth Buechley, is a serial-entrepreneur and business founder who has led several multi-million dollar exits. In his most recent role as President of SOL-iD USA (www.solid.com), he helped bring cellular and public safety radio coverage to some of the most recognized venues in America, including the Empire State Building, the NY Subway, Moscone Center, and Daytona International Speedway. He has served and negotiated contracts with leading global organizations such as Nike, Amazon, Kaiser Permanente, AT&T, Verizon, T-Mobile, and Sprint.

He is the founder of the Safer Building Coalition (www.saferbuildings.org) and the co-founder of Priority RF (www.priorityrf.com), a business focused on funding and managing in-building technology infrastructure.

An experienced keynote speaker and emcee, Seth is a member of Young President Organization (YPO) and the President of Legacy, LLC, his platform for writing, speaking, and coaching the next generation of leaders. He and his wife, Helen, live in Roseburg, Oregon, enjoying the rural Pacific Northwest while raising their four children.

Visit www.sethbuechley.com to keep updated or to inquire about booking Seth for a speaking or coaching engagement.

ACKNOWLEDGMENTS

I'd like to thank my wife, Helen Buechley, for her patience and adjustment to having me around the house physically while I was mentally consumed with writing. She has been the guardrail to my driven personality for over 25 years. Without her presence…well, I hate to even think. I'm grateful to my business partners, Bryan Kemper and Chip Laughton, for giving me a chance to serve and grow in a high-stakes role. I want to recognize Rick Graham, my leadership coach for many years who encouraged me to push into new areas and to trust God in the middle of the stormy seas. I want to thank the executive team at SOLiD USA; Ken Sandfeld, Mike Collado, Hitesh Kshatriya, Dennis Rigney, Barry Bruce, and Eric Carey for their willingness to do the work required to become a cohesive team and providing a testbed for leading with gratitude.

And, finally, I'd like to thank the entire team at Elevate Publishing, particularly my editor, Anna McHargue, for their skill and effort spent guiding me through the process of writing and bringing a book to market.